DATE DUE

			PRINTED IN U.S.A.

ISSUES THAT CONCERN YOU

Dropping Out of School

Heidi Watkins, *Book Editor*

GREENHAVEN PRESS
A part of Gale, Cengage Learning

GALE
CENGAGE Learning·

Detroit • New York • San Francisco • New Haven, Conn • Waterville, Maine • London

Elizabeth Des Chenes, *Director, Publishing Solutions*

For more information, contact:
Greenhaven Press
27500 Drake Rd.
Farmington Hills, MI 48331-3535
Or you can visit our Internet site at gale.cengage.com

For product information and technology assistance, contact us at

Gale Customer Support, 1-800-877-4253
For permission to use material from this text or product, submit all requests online at
www.cengage.com/permissions

Further permissions questions can be e-mailed to permissionrequest@cengage.com

Articles in Greenhaven Press anthologies are often edited for length to meet page requirements. In addition, original titles of these works are changed to clearly present the main thesis and to explicitly indicate the author's opinion. Every effort is made to ensure that Greenhaven Press accurately reflects the original intent of the authors. Every effort has been made to trace the owners of copyrighted material.

Cover image © Gemenacom/Shutterstock.com

LIBRARY OF CONGRESS CATALOGING-IN-PUBLICATION DATA

Dropping out of school / Heidi Watkins, book editor.
    p. cm. -- (Issues that concern you)
  Summary: "Dropping Out of School: This series provides readers with information on topics of current interest. Focusing on important social issues, each anthology examines its subject in a variety of ways, from personal accounts to factual articles"--Provided by publisher.
  Includes bibliographical references and index.
  ISBN 978-0-7377-6289-1 (hardback)
  1. Dropouts--United States--Juvenile literature. 2. Dropouts--United States--Attitudes--Juvenile literature. 3. Dropouts--United States--Social conditions--Juvenile literature. I. Watkins, Heidi.
  LC143.D77 2012
  371.2913--dc23
                                                          2012021470

Printed in the United States of America
1 2 3 4 5 6 7 16 15 14 13 12

CONTENTS

Chanratta Som skipped class frequently, leading to his expulsion from high school at age seventeen. He recalls regretfully, "I didn't like school. . . . But as you get older, you start to understand that it's really important." Monica Fontanez dropped out of high school twice and has since been unable to find work. "Wherever I went, there were no openings,"[1] she tells a writer for the *Christian Science Monitor*.

Like many other high school dropouts (an estimated 1.2 million a year), Chanratta and Monica are facing the harsh reality of a lost education. Since dropping out, however, Chanratta has passed the General Educational Development (GED) exam, earning him a general equivalency diploma (also called a GED) and is now optimistic about the future. Monica hopes to finish her GED before her baby is born and is looking forward to a better life for herself and her child.

Since its inception, the GED has been synonymous with the hope for a second chance for students like Chanratta and Monica. Established in the 1940s to meet the needs of World War II veterans, it has been considered the equivalent of a high school diploma—proof for potential employers and college admissions counselors that the recipient has mastered high school level skills in reading, writing, math, science, and social studies. Recently, however, some educators have been wondering whether the GED is actually harming the education system in America, sugar-coating the idea of dropping out, epitomized in the all-too-common phrase, "I'll just get my GED."

GED students Carlos and Melinda, quoted in an article in *City Journal*, are typical. "I saw some friends get their GED and I thought: 'Why should I stay around here?'" says Carlos. When Melinda's family was about to lose their van, her reaction was, "No way: that's our van," she remembers. "I told my mom that I was going to work so we could keep it. She told me not to, but I said it was okay—I could always get my GED." A few years later,

Carlos is still without that GED. "I should've stayed in school," he says. "It's hard coming back after being out of the routine, and I've forgotten a bunch of stuff."[2] Seven years later, Melinda is starting a GED prep program for the third time, quitting the first two times because she was exhausted after long days working in a copy shop.

The idea that the existence of the GED gives students an excuse to drop out of high school is supported by more than these stories. A study by the Urban Institute indicates that the easier it is to get a GED in a state, the higher the dropout rate in that state. Indeed, the percentage of test takers who are only in their teens has been increasing over the last few decades as more and more states are allowing younger dropouts to benefit from the test, dropping age restrictions from eighteen to sixteen. In fact, between 1978 and 2008, the number of teen test takers increased from 31 percent to 41 percent, peaking in 2002 at 49 percent, according to figures from the US National Center for Educational Statistics. Even more disconcerting is the fact that thousands of students never even attempt the test. "They drop out thinking, oh this will be easy," says Duncan Chaplin, senior researcher with Mathematica Policy Research, but "they just don't get around to it."[3]

Educators and researchers are not just worried that the prospect of a GED is making the idea of leaving high school more tempting but are voicing concerns that once completed, a GED is not the fix that students like Chanratta and Monica expect it to be. "The GED is a credential. Is it adequate for gainful employment and a living wage in the United States of America today? I do not think so,"[4] says Los Angeles school superintendent John Deasy in a February 2012 *Weekend Edition* interview on National Public Radio.

Superintendent Deasy's concern is not unfounded. According to 2009 figures from the US Census Bureau, while the average GED recipient does earn more than the average high school dropout ($3,100 versus $2,400 per month, respectively), the traditional high school graduate earns much more ($4,700 per month).

A student takes a GED test. Since its inception in the 1940s, GED tests have been a second chance to get the equivalent of a high school diploma.

Neither does earning a bachelor's degree after completing the GED even out the average monthly earnings. On average, someone with a high school diploma plus a bachelor's degree makes $6,300 per month, while someone with a GED plus a bachelor's degree only makes about $4,900 per month.

Furthermore, according to the Census Bureau, a high school graduate is also more likely to earn a bachelor's degree or even go to college in the first place. About three-quarters of all high school graduates, six years later, had completed some education past high school (74 percent) compared with less than half of GED graduates (43 percent). Even more striking is the contrast between college graduation rates. About 33 percent of high school graduates complete a college degree versus about 5 percent of GED graduates. In fact, less than half of GED earners even return for a second semester of college.

These concerns are why the GED exam is about to get a makeover. Beginning January 1, 2014, the current GED will be a thing of the past. "We are developing a GED test in the future which will point toward more information for employers and colleges and individuals about the basic skills that they have and at what level have they mastered them,"[5] says Nicole Chestang, vice president of the GED Testing Service.

The new tests will be entirely computer-based and will be more difficult. For example, in the essay portion, instead of writing about themselves or an idea, test takers will be required to analyze and cite evidence from a passage that they are given. The math and science portions will also require more analytical skills, the math test will include more word problems, and the science and social studies tests will include far more graphs and charts. An additional essay will be required in the social studies test as well.

While these changes are in line with preparing students for the workforce and higher education and will hopefully encourage high school students to stay in school, they also pose concerns. Adults without any computer skills will especially be affected, for example. The role of the GED in the school dropout crisis is just one of the issues related to whether to stay in school that students face today. Authors in this anthology examine dropping out of school across a wide spectrum. In addition, the volume contains several appendixes to help the reader understand and further explore the topic, including a thorough bibliography and a list of organizations to contact for further information. The appendix titled "What You Should Know About Dropping Out of School" offers facts and statistics. The appendix "What You Should Do About Dropping Out of School" offers tips for young people. With all these features, *Issues That Concern You: Dropping Out of School* provides an excellent resource for everyone interested in this troubling issue.

Notes

1. Quoted in Stacy Teicher Khadaroo, "Why GED Classes Are Full," *Christian Science Monitor*, June 7, 2009.
2. Quoted in Jay P. Greene, "GEDs Aren't Worth the Paper They Are Printed On," *City Journal*, Winter 2002. www.city-journal .org/html/12_1_geds_arent.html.
3. Quoted in Nathan Thornburgh, "Does the GED Really Do the Job?," *Time*, April 11, 2006.
4. Quoted in Claudio Sanchez, "In Today's Economy, How Far Can a GED Take You?," NPR *Weekend Edition*, February 18, 2012. www.npr.org/2012/02/18/147015513/in-todays-economy -how-far-can-a-ged-take-you.
5. Quoted in Sanchez, "In Today's Economy, How Far Can a GED Take You?"

ONE

Dropping Out of School Is a National Crisis

Keith Melville

Led by the Pew Partnership for Civic Change, Learning to Finish is a community-based effort established to address the school dropout crisis. This viewpoint is an excerpt of a report written by Keith Melville, a scholar who has written extensively about research on public problems. Melville explains the dropout crisis and how it has reached epidemic proportions. The extent of the crisis, the difficulty of measuring the true number of high school dropouts, and the impact of low graduation rates upon the entire public are among the points of discussion.

Imagine a nationwide epidemic so severe that it strikes one in three teenagers and so malignant that few ever recover from it. The epidemic results in cascading costs for communities and for the nation as a whole—an estimated $200 to $300 billion to cover the cost of those struck by this affliction each year. If such an epidemic existed, you would assume it would be front-page news, a top-of-the-agenda item for public action.

Such an epidemic already exists. Although it is apparent in most communities, it is, in the words of *New York Times* columnist Bob Herbert, "an under-recognized, underreported crisis in

Keith Melville, "The Dropout Epidemic," *The School Dropout Crisis: Why One-Third of All High School Students Don't Graduate and What You Can Do About It*, 2006, pp. 4–9. www.pew-partnership.org. Copyright © 2006 by The University of Richmond Pew Partnership for Civic Change. All rights reserved. Excerpted and reproduced by permission.

American life." The problem is that large numbers of students drop out before finishing high school, with devastating consequences for them personally and for their communities.

A recent report from the Educational Testing Service (ETS) entitled *One-Third of a Nation* is one in a series of sobering assessments which underline the extent of the problem. For the nation as a whole, only about two-thirds of all students who enter 9th grade graduate with a regular diploma four years later. Among poor, black, and Latino youngsters, the likelihood that they will graduate is even smaller. In 2004, according to a report co-authored by the Urban Institute and the Civil Rights Project at Harvard University, only 50 percent of black students, 51 percent of Native Americans, and 53 percent of Hispanic students graduated from high school. Among African-American, Hispanic, and Native American males, the rates are even lower.

A Community Problem

The public schools are intended as a ladder of opportunity, a way of gaining the knowledge needed to make one's way in a society that doesn't have much to offer those who are uneducated and unskilled. Unlike the situation that existed until several decades ago, when uneducated but energetic young adults could work their way up to decent jobs and satisfying lives, almost all businesses today need workers with skills that presume at least a high school diploma. Individuals without a high school diploma aren't regarded as prime recruits for the US military, and they typically don't qualify even for low-wage positions in fast-food restaurants.

In the words of educational researchers Robert Balfanz and Nettie Legters, "From Benton Harbor to Los Angeles, from Akron to San Antonio, from Chicago's south side to rural North Carolina, close to half of the students in these communities do not graduate from high school, let alone leave high school prepared to fully participate in civic life. It is no coincidence that these locales are gripped by high rates of unemployment, crime, ill health, and chronic despair. For many people in these and other areas, the only real and lasting pipeline out of poverty in modern

America, a solid high school education followed by postsecondary schooling, is cracked and leaking."

Difficult to Measure

There is some dispute among educational researchers about the extent of the problem and whether it is getting worse. To determine precisely how many students graduate, it would be necessary to assign lifetime ID numbers to permit researchers to track students, follow them when they move, and determine how many actually complete a diploma. Since that has not been done, no assessment of the dropout problem is entirely accurate, and there are significant differences depending on who you ask. By some indications, graduation rates have not changed much in recent years.

Most recent reports, however, tell a different story. Whether you consult research that examines schools with "weak promoting power" or overall assessments such as the ETS report, many reports show that the problem is worse than it was generally recognized to be, and that the situation has deteriorated in recent years. It appears that high school completion rates have declined in most states since 1990. Even at a time when there has been sustained attention to improving school performance and accountability, remarks Paul Barton, author of the ETS report, "this is a story of losing ground."

For all the good intentions behind a much-discussed federal education act called "No Child Left Behind," the fact is that many students in the United States are still left behind and never catch up. Part of the reason we continue to lose ground is that the dropout problem attracts nowhere near the attention it deserves. Roughly one million American teenagers walk away from high school each year before they graduate, setting out on a path that for most of them is a dead end.

Selective Epidemic

While dropouts are a problem almost everywhere, even in communities that pride themselves on having a high percentage of college-bound kids, this epidemic does not affect all communities equally. Completion rates vary from one state to another, from a high of 88 percent to a low of 48 percent as a state-wide average. The Midwestern states and the Northeast have the highest graduation rates, while the dropout rate is highest in the South.

Males drop out somewhat more often than females, but gender differences are not very large. Males and females do, however, tend to give different reasons for dropping out. Young

In the United States about two-thirds of all students who enter ninth grade ultimately receive a high school diploma.

women most often drop out due to pregnancy and marriage, as well as academic difficulties. Young men more often drop out because of behavioral problems or because they are seeking employment.

The pattern of school dropouts—like many social problems—tends to reflect the economic and racial make-up of communities. Graduation rates for white and Asian students are higher than the national average, with completion rates for the two groups at 75 and 77 percent respectively. In their own right, these statistics are troubling since they show that even among the most advantaged groups, one in four students drops out.

The dropout problem is most serious among blacks, Hispanics, and American-Indian students, barely half of whom graduate from high school. In Bob Herbert's words, "Far from preparing kids for college, big-city high schools in neighborhoods with large numbers of poor, black, or Latino youngsters are just hemorrhaging students. The kids are vanishing into a wilderness of ignorance."

Some researchers use the phrase "weak promoting power" to describe high schools with a severe dropout problem—the 2,000 or so schools where fewer than 6 in 10 students graduate. These schools are more vividly and accurately characterized as "dropout factories," to use Robert Balfanz's phrase. Representing about one-fifth of all high schools nationally, these schools—typically located in large cities, in nearly every state—are where the dropout problem exists in its most concentrated form. Students who enter many of these schools—attended by nearly half of the country's African-American students and 40 percent of its Latino students—are more likely to drop out than they are to receive a diploma.

Risks and Rewards

Reports about the nation's schools often refer to "at risk" kids who are on the verge of dropping out. When you look at what happens to those who drop out, you realize how real the risk is—both in the years immediately after they leave school and as they get older. The headline on dozens of studies of teenagers who leave high school is that dropouts have only a slim chance of succeeding, earning a decent wage, or achieving a stable and productive life.

Even dropouts who manage to get work are on a downhill slide. Because few job openings exist for those who don't have a high school diploma, the economic prospects for dropouts are much bleaker than they were several decades ago. Most are unable to get jobs that pay enough to keep them out of poverty. They earn about $150 a week less, on average, compared to high school graduates, and are three times more likely to live in poverty.

That is more than a short-term problem. Years after they leave school, dropouts are far more likely to be stuck in low-wage jobs or chronically unemployed. One study that looked at 20- to 24-year-olds who had not completed high school—people who are in the early marriage and childbearing years—found that fewer than 6 in 10 are employed.

With no good prospect for decent paying work, it is not surprising that dropouts are far more likely—compared to those who finish high school—to be unmarried or divorced, and more likely to be on public assistance. They are also far more likely to end up on the wrong side of the law. Drawing on Department of Justice data, the author of a 2003 study found that more than two-thirds of all inmates are dropouts, and that almost half of all African-American men who drop out of high school have a prison record by the time they are in their early 30s.

Community Consequences

If you think dropping out is mainly an individual choice and that those who left school are paying a personal price for a bad decision, think about the consequences for the community. Because of the loss of their efforts in the labor force, the loss of their taxes, plus the burden of paying for public assistance and prisons, every dropout represents a costly public liability. At a recent conference at Columbia University's Teacher's College, educational researchers gathered to compare studies

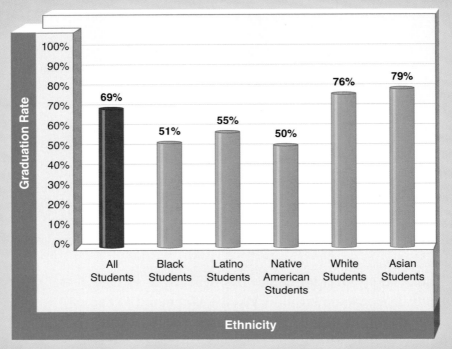

of the public impact of the dropout problem. They noted that dropouts comprise nearly half of the heads of households on welfare, and that each year's new class of dropouts will cost taxpayers more than $200 billion over the course of their lifetimes in lost earnings and tax revenues, not to mention the cost of the social services they require. . . .

Dealing with the dropout crisis is a matter of allocating sufficient resources and recognizing what is at stake when students drop out. As educational researcher Gary Orfield notes, "It is depressing to realize that many of the 'dropout factories' that send hundreds of students off a figurative cliff each year don't have as much money to spend on dropout intervention as it will cost to keep even one of their dropouts in prison for a year."

It is also, as Orfield points out, a matter of how we choose to regard high school dropouts. "If we start thinking about students who drop out as people who have potential instead of as threats to society, we will have to recognize the challenges they are facing and the incredible losses sustained in communities where most of these people have no future. If we are to benefit from their talents, we must help them finish school and give them a chance to succeed as adults in this society."

TWO

The Dropout Crisis Is Also an Economic Crisis

Jeff Kelly Lowenstein and Sarah Karp

The *Chicago Reporter* is an investigative monthly magazine, reporting on social, economic, and political issues. This viewpoint is the fourth and final article in a series about educational funding published in the *Chicago Reporter*. Written by Jeff Kelly Lowenstein, now a frequent writer for the *Huffington Post*, and Sarah Karp, an award-winning journalist, it examines the economic impact of high school dropouts: the millions of tax dollars spent to financially support unemployed dropouts, the decreased tax revenue resulting from such unemployment, as well as the increased crime and incarceration costs associated with high school dropouts.

One winter day during his junior year at Harlan High School in the Roseland neighborhood [of Chicago] Donte Webb and his buddies left the school building but decided to go back when they got chilly. Upon their return, they were met by an administrator who issued suspensions.

At the end of that school year, Webb left the school building for good. He never went back to Harlan, or any other school, for his senior year. "I got distracted," said Webb, who described himself as a punk of a teenager who smoked weed everyday and didn't really take an interest in school.

His homeroom teacher had told him to get serious about his class work. But he was too wrapped up in "hanging out" to listen to her, said Webb, now 20. "Instead of doing what I should have been doing, I was doing other things."

Webb's wrong turn has cost him dearly. And research shows that it will also cost the rest of us.

In 2005, the "social costs," for nearly 880,000 Illinois residents without a high school diploma or GED [general equivalency diploma], was close to $10 billion, according to one researcher. Those costs include more than $9 billion in reduced earnings and lower state and federal tax contributions. It also includes nearly $1 billion more in expenses for prisons, health care and various forms of public assistance, according to research by Andrew Sum, an economics professor at Northeastern University in Boston.

In January 2002, the Illinois State Board of Education noted that 50 percent of Illinois welfare recipients, at that time, were high school dropouts, and that 30 percent of state prison inmates could not read at a sixth grade level. "The consequences of failing to bring all students to a high level of achievement are significant," the board wrote.

School Funding and Social Outcomes

Some scholars argue that it makes more sense to invest in school interventions for children while they're in elementary school and high school rather than paying many times more in social programs and diminished tax dollars once children have dropped out of school. Chicago neighborhoods with the highest percentages of adults without a diploma or GED, particularly some black and Latino areas, bear the brunt of joblessness and poverty, according to an analysis of census data.

Although the exact relationship between school funding and social outcomes is murky, the substantial costs that dropouts generate are clear, according to Henry M. Levin, a professor

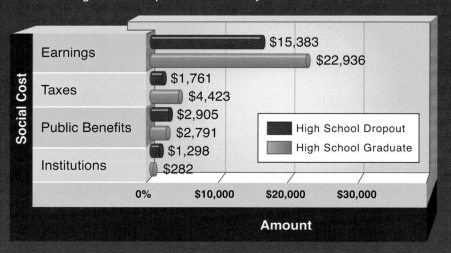

Costly Choices: Social Costs in Illinois, 2005

Research shows that high school dropouts have greater "social costs" than high school graduates because, on average, dropouts earn less, pay less in taxes and rely more heavily on public benefits and institutions. In 2005 the combined costs for 880,000 Illinois residents without a high school diploma was nearly $10 billion.

Social Cost

Earnings — High School Dropout: $15,383 / High School Graduate: $22,936
Taxes — $1,761 / $4,423
Public Benefits — $2,905 / $2,791
Institutions — $1,298 / $282

0% $10,000 $20,000 $30,000

Amount

High School Dropout
High School Graduate

of economics and education at Teachers College at Columbia University in New York City. "Even though many of us may feel that we are unaffected by the massive educational inequities in our society, the facts are just the opposite," said Levin, who has studied the economics of education, including social costs analyses, for almost 40 years. "We all pay for such failure, and the costs are staggering."

Dropouts Cost Everyone

According to Sum, by dropping out of high school, Webb is costing himself an average of close to $8,000 a year in earnings—or nearly $355,000 over the course of his lifetime.

Webb said he remained directionless after he dropped out. He tried to find work but was unable to. His low point came when he got caught in a stolen car and landed in Cook County Jail for three long days and three long nights. "That is the worst place ever," he said.

For that offense, Webb got probation.

But the lower wages and higher unemployment rates also result in costs for everyone, according to Sum, director of the Center for Labor Market Studies at Northeastern University.

While dropouts paid an average of $1,761 in state and federal taxes in 2005, graduates paid $4,423—a difference of close to $2,700. For nearly 880,000 in Illinois without a diploma or GED, in 2005, the "losses" totaled nearly $6.65 billion in earnings and $2.34 billion in state and federal taxes.

The costs were not limited to earnings and taxes.

Sum estimated that dropouts collected an average of $2,905 in public benefits in 2005—about $114 more than graduates. These include costs for health programs like Medicare and Medicaid, public assistance, food stamps and unemployment.

In addition, dropouts were more likely to be found in prison and public mental health facilities, according to Sum. He estimated that the average cost for these two institutions was about $1,300 for male dropouts, compared with about $300 for male graduates.

Counting the lost wages and taxes and the additional public expenses in 2005, the price tag for dropouts was a whopping $9.98 billion, according to Sum's research.

Projected over a lifetime, from ages 18 to 64, the "social costs" for each dropout is more than $533,000, according to Sum.

Some researchers have questioned the precision of social cost analyses. But most agree that a diploma could improve the quality of life for most dropouts. "At every level of job, the higher your educational attainment, the lower your level of unemployment and the more likely you are to receive a good wage," said Ralph Martire of the Center for Tax and Budget Accountability, a Chicago-based economic policy think tank.

Wiyvonne Rivers has lived it. It's been more than a decade since Rivers—at 16 and pregnant—dropped out of high school.

In the years since, she has worked at numerous places—from fast food restaurants to warehouses to stuffing envelopes in offices. "I have never stopped trying to do better," she said.

But most of those positions paid minimum wage or a little higher, and they were unstable positions. Rivers said she would either get laid off or she'd tire of the jobs and quit.

When she couldn't find work, she'd go on welfare. But making ends meet on public assistance is also difficult. "I get tired of struggling," she said.

Not only are Rivers and other dropouts affected, but so is the state's future economic vitality, Martire said. "To attract better businesses in Illinois [you have to ask], 'Does the state produce the type of worker that you need?'" he said. "If the answer is, 'No,' the kind of job growth you are going to get is the jobs that pay less and have fewer benefits. One of the reasons is that's the kind of workforce you are producing."

Rivers feels badly that her daughter, now 11, is growing up in the same poverty that she did. She tries to tell her the importance of staying in school. "I tell her to make different choices," Rivers said. "I try to tell her to endure."

Proven Prevention Strategies

Several researchers, including Levin, believe that Illinois can turn things around with greater investments in proven dropout reduction strategies, like Chicago's child-parent centers, dropout prevention programs, smaller class sizes in elementary schools and higher teacher salaries to attract more high-quality instructors.

Levin said research has shown that these interventions lead to higher high school graduation rates and, as a result, a savings in "social costs."

Of these interventions, Levin found that dropout prevention yielded the greatest "savings." Every dollar spent in dropout prevention led to a $3.50 reduction in social costs, Levin said. "Throwing money at the problem is not the solution; it's putting money into targeted strategies that's important."

More of these interventions could be on the way in Illinois.

Statistics show that dropouts are more likely to end up in prison and public mental health facilities.

In October 2006, Gov. Rod Blagojevich launched a task force to focus on re-enrolling high school dropouts. The task force will hold hearings throughout the state before issuing an interim report in January 2007 and a final report in January 2008. And Illinois Senate President Emil Jones Jr. said he would be poised to act on the task force's recommendations. "Many young people are falling off the cliff," said Jones, noting that 62 percent of prison inmates in Illinois are high school dropouts. "Society pays a hell of a price when we do not provide a safety net, when we do not pull them back so that they can become productive citizens in our society."

Darien Haywood, 17, is an example of what can happen when dropouts are pulled back. He now attends Olive-Harvey Middle College, an alternative high school located on the Far South Side.

Thanks to his own efforts and the school's small and supportive environment, Haywood has become an honors student and student council president, with plans to become a plastic surgeon.

Haywood, who began gangbanging and selling drugs when he was 12, is certain that he was headed toward prison or death before the program allowed him to make a U-turn. And there are many others like him, Haywood said. "A lot of them want to take that step, but they're scared to be a leader."

Both Webb and Rivers are taking those scary steps.

They've attended pre-GED and GED classes in an old Hyde Park neighborhood mansion on the South Side. The classes are provided by the Blue Gargoyle, an organization providing education, counseling and employment services among its three South Side locations.

Rivers came to the program . . . for help with the GED test. For years, she's been taking classes to prepare for the test, but she hasn't passed it.

Webb's outlook changed after meeting a South Side minister, who became a father figure to him and encouraged him to go back to school. Webb now wants to go to college and become a social worker. "He told me that my future would not be too much without an education," he said.

THREE

The Dropout Crisis Is Improving

Sarah D. Sparks

> "Dropout Factories" are high schools that have been iden-
> tified as graduating less than 60 percent of incoming ninth
> graders four years later. In this viewpoint, Sarah D. Sparks,
> an education research reporter for *Education Week*, high-
> lights the results of a 2011 study that concluded that the
> number of these underperforming high schools is declin-
> ing. Sparks reports that the positive change is attributed
> to growing concerns over an increasingly competitive
> global workforce, increased institutional accountability
> combined with the standardization of measurement meth-
> ods, and multiple efforts by states and school districts to
> improve graduation rates.

After decades of flat-lining graduation rates, states finally
have started to turn around or close hundreds of so-called
"dropout factory" schools and recover some of the thousands of
students who had already given up, according to a new study.

The Washington [D.C.]-based policy firm Civic Enterprises,
whose 2006 report, "The Silent Epidemic," helped galvanize state
and federal attention on high school dropouts, reported last week
[in late November/early December 2010] that most states have

gained momentum in improving graduation rates, but will need to improve at least five times faster to meet a national goal of 90 percent of students graduating on time by 2020.

The study suggests that a combination of state economic concerns and federal accountability pressure has helped drive up the national graduation rate from 72 percent in 2001 to 75 percent in 2008, the most recent federal graduation estimate. Black, Hispanic, and Native American students made some of the great-

Some schools, such as this one in Indiana, have improved their graduation rates by implementing tutoring programs for struggling students.

est gains, but more than 40 percent of those students still did not graduate on time as of 2008.

It also finds that the number of high schools that graduate 60 percent or fewer of their incoming 9th graders four years later—the so-called "dropout factories," which account for fully half of the students who leave school each year—has declined from 2,007 schools in 2002 to 1,746 in 2008.

In the report, the study's authors—John M. Bridgeland, the chief executive officer of Civic Enterprises; Laura A. Moore, the organization's program and policy manager for youth development; Director Robert Balfanz and Deputy Director Joanna H. Fox of the Everyone Graduates Center at Johns Hopkins University in Baltimore; and the America's Promise Alliance, a Washington group started by former U.S. Secretary of State Colin Powell—call for a "Civic Marshall Plan" to reconstruct the nation's high schools as comprehensively as the Allies planned to rebuild Europe after World War II.

The plan advises all states to follow the best practices of states such as Tennessee, which had a 15 percent graduation-rate increase, and New York, where the numbers of students graduating on time rose by 10 percent over the 2001–2008 study period. These include targeting schools with high dropout rates and the lower grades that feed into them; providing more-rigorous course requirements along with more flexible class schedules for students; and developing early-warning systems to identify students in earlier grades at risk of dropping out. It also tailors specific strategies for each state to enable them to reach the 90 percent graduation goal.

"Most states did one or two or three things together, but it's the places that weave multiple things together that made the biggest progress," Mr. Bridgeland said. "It's not just saying, 'Do it better,' but saying, 'We can help you do a more comprehensive approach to get bigger impacts.'"

Converging Forces

Mr. Bridgeland said there is greater political will to increase graduation rates now, both because the economic crisis has increased concern about global job competitiveness and because 2008 changes to federal education grants require that states and districts report graduation rates using a uniform longitudinal measure that tracks individual students from 8th grade through graduation.

"I would just tell you the phones are ringing off the hook from states and districts that are waking up to the fact that they have to meet these graduation-rate-reporting requirements and annual targets for AYP," Mr. Bridgeland said. The latter reference is to the federal No Child Left Behind law's mandate for schools to make "adequate yearly progress" on state tests each year.

The new measure, called the adjusted cohort-graduation rate, must be reported beginning in the 2010–11 school year, and states and districts will be accountable for meeting annual improvement targets using the measure beginning in 2011–12.

"It's not just accountability, but the requirement that everyone calculates the graduation rate in the same way; it's similar to what the NAEP [National Assessment of Educational Progress] does in leveling the playing field," Ms. Fox said. "You can't pull the wool over anybody's eyes anymore by saying, 'We have a 90 percent grad rate,' when you have schools that have a 50 percent graduation rate."

For this study, however, researchers used existing U.S. Department of Education estimates for calculating cohort graduation rates for the nation as a whole.

The 261-school decline in the numbers of high schools classified as "dropout factories," drawn from data gathered by the Everyone Graduates Center, doesn't tell the whole story. Seven hundred new schools were identified during that time even as 900 previously identified schools turned themselves around. Southern states made the most progress, accounting for 216 of the schools that improved enough to get off the list.

"The South has been very poor for very long, and Southern governors have seen education as a real economic imperative," said Ms. Fox of the Everyone Graduates Center. The turned-around schools in that region seemed to have more "stick-to-itiveness" than those where dropout rates remained low, she said.

Number of "Dropout Factories" in the United States

Year	Total Number of High Schools*	High Schools Graduating Less than 60% of Students	
		Percentage of High Schools	Number of High Schools
Class of 1993	10,296	12%	1,254
Class of 1996	10,709	16%	1,717
Class of 1999	10,915	18%	1,968
Class of 2002	11,129	18%	2,007
Class of 2005	11,800	15%	1,766
Class of 2008	12,074	14%	1,746

*Regular and vocational high schools with more than 300 students whose first class entered no later than 2004–2005.

Taken from: Robert Balfanz, John M. Bridgeland, Laura A. Moore, and Joanna Horning Fox, "Building a Grad Nation: Progress and Challenge in Ending the High School Dropout Epidemic," November 2010, p. 25.

"They kept trying different things. If something didn't work, they modified it again."

For example, Mr. Bridgeland and Ms. Fox attributed Tennessee's improvement to comprehensive reforms, such as training and distributing 100 "exemplary educators" to coach and lead instruction in high-need high schools while toughening graduation content requirements and conducting school-by-school monitoring and improvement plans for the worst high schools. The state even required students under 18 to attend school or graduate in order to get a driver's license.

While some education watchers have voiced concern that increasing education standards could make it harder for students falling behind in high school to catch up and graduate, Mr. Balfanz said the research showed "the exact opposite: increasing their standards and requirements improved graduation rates. It's exactly what the dropouts had said they wanted: more rigor; to be challenged."

Recovering Students

Alabama, another state that succeeded in raising school completion rates, based its graduation initiatives on a series of surveys of students who had already dropped out of the system, according to Tommy Bice, the state's deputy superintendent of education. "For years, we had attempted to re-engage students in school, but we were attempting to re-engage them in a system that hadn't worked to start with," he said. "I think the reason we've been able to make some significant moves is we've started listening to our students. We started seeing things that were policy driven that, if changed, would make it easier for students to come back."

The state ramped up its graduation requirements but based mastery on skills tests rather than Carnegie units of credit or seat time. It also expanded credit-recovery programs to provide more support for students. The Mobile school district, for example, has re-enrolled more than 500 students who had left school in the past year through "drop-back-in academies" set up in neighborhood centers and empty storefronts. These allowed students to schedule their own school hours around work and family care, Mr. Bice said.

This school year, the state also plans to join Louisiana and South Carolina in launching a statewide longitudinal student data system that can flag predictors of dropout risk in elementary school. These early indicators include absenteeism, behavior problems, and failing core classes, such as mathematics and reading.

Such systems are critical, Mr. Bridgeland said, because even the more-accurate graduation rate methods come too late, rendering them "basically autopsy reports on these students."

Individual schools already are using such early-warning systems as part of their turnaround plans. The Feltonville School of Arts and Sciences, a middle school that has been a feeder for high-risk high schools in Philadelphia, implemented a student-tracking system as part of the Diplomas Now initiative piloted by Mr. Balfanz. . . .

The system allowed teachers to identify and target students with recurring absences or academic or behavior problems, all of which can predict high school dropout risk. The school partnered with community groups such as City Year and Communities in Schools to provide additional help to those students. Within a year, the number of students failing core subjects dropped by 80 percent in reading and 83 percent in math; the number of students missing 20 percent of class or more dropped by more than half. Diplomas Now has since received a federal grant to replicate the program in other high-dropout schools and their feeder schools.

"We think these [early warning systems] can be a big additional lever to mobilize resources to help these students," Mr. Bridgeland said.

FOUR

High School Dropouts Are More Severely Affected by a Poor Economy than Graduates

Alliance for Excellent Education

The fact that the average high school dropout earns less over his or her lifetime than the typical high school graduate is well documented. According to a 2011 study, the economic recession significantly increases this disparity. This viewpoint by the Alliance for Excellent Education, an organization that advocates for increased education funding and high school reform in an effort to increase high school graduation rates, details the differences in earnings and explains how high unemployment rates disproportionately affect those with less education, especially high school dropouts in particular.

Every school day, nearly 7,000 students become dropouts. Annually, that adds up to about 1.2 million students who will not graduate from high school with their peers as scheduled. Lacking a high school diploma, these individuals will be far more likely than graduates to spend their lives periodically unemployed, on government assistance, or cycling in and out of the prison system.

Most high school dropouts see the result of their decision to leave school very clearly in the slimness of their wallets. The average annual income for a high school dropout in 2009 was $19,540, compared to $27,380 for a high school graduate, a difference of $7,840. The impact on the country's economy is less visible, but cumulatively its effect is staggering.

If the nation's secondary schools improved sufficiently to graduate all of their students, rather than the 72 percent of students who currently graduate annually, the payoff would be significant. For instance, if the students who dropped out of the Class of 2011 had graduated, the nation's economy would likely benefit from nearly $154 billion in additional income over the course of their lifetimes.

Everyone benefits from increased graduation rates. The graduates themselves, on average, will earn higher wages and enjoy more comfortable and secure lifestyles. At the same time, the nation benefits from their increased purchasing power, collects higher tax receipts, and sees higher levels of worker productivity.

Economic Recession and High School Dropouts

Not only do employed high school dropouts earn less than employed high school graduates, high school dropouts are much more likely to be unemployed during economic downturns. Since the economic recession began in December 2007, the national unemployment rate has gone from 5 percent to 9.1 percent in August 2011.

The unemployment rate for individuals of all education levels has skyrocketed since December 2007, but high school dropouts have faced the most difficulty with finding a job. According to data from the U.S. Bureau of Labor Statistics, the unemployment rate for high school dropouts in August 2011—four years after the start of the recession—was 14.3 percent, compared to 9.6 percent for high school graduates, 8.2 percent for individuals with some college credits or an associate's degree, and 4.3 percent for individuals with a bachelor's degree or higher.

Students Who Learn More Earn More

Recent research conducted by the Alliance for Excellent Education in partnership with Economic Modeling Specialists, Inc., an Idaho-based economic modeling firm, provides a look at the additional earnings an individual would likely expect over the course of his or her lifetime by completing high school. This analysis is based upon state-specific economic data that reflects the postrecession economic reality.

The calculations . . . show the monetary benefits each state would likely accrue over the lifetimes of just one year's worth of dropouts if those students had graduated. Calculations are based on the number of dropouts and average earnings by education level, which causes the numbers to vary from state to state:

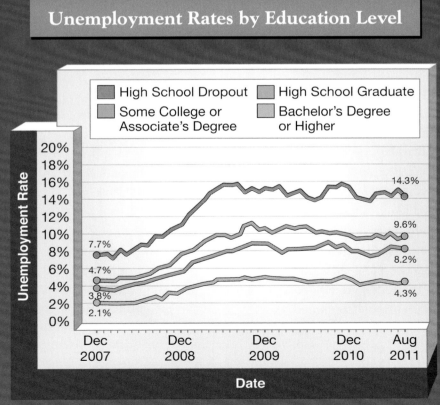

Unemployment Rates by Education Level

Vermont (at the low end) would likely see its economy increase by $147 million; Massachusetts (near the middle) would likely add $2 billion to its economy, and California's economy (at the high end) would likely accrue an additional $21 billion over the lifetimes of just one year's worth of dropouts if those students had graduated. These figures are conservative and do not take into account the added economic growth generated from each new dollar put into the economy.

All told, these additional earnings from a single high school class would likely pour a total of $154 billion into the national economy. Unless high schools are able to graduate their students at higher rates, nearly 12 million students will likely drop out over the next decade, resulting in a loss to the nation of *$1.5 trillion.*

More High School Graduates Benefit Society

Obviously, dropouts are a drain on the nation's economy and the economies of each state. Lower local, state, and national tax revenues are the most obvious consequence of higher dropout rates; even when dropouts are employed, they earn significantly lower wages than do graduates. State and local economies suffer further when they have less-educated populaces, as they find it more difficult to attract new business investment. Simultaneously, these entities must spend more on social programs when their populations have lower educational levels.

The nation's economy and competitive standing also suffer when there are high dropout rates. Among developed countries, the United States ranks twenty-first in high school graduation rates and fifteenth in college attainment rates among twenty-five- to thirty-four-year-olds. Dropouts represent a tremendous loss of human potential and productivity, and they significantly reduce the nation's ability to compete in an increasingly global economy. Furthermore, recent estimates project that the future domestic workforce demands will require higher levels of education among U.S. workers. However, without significant improvements in the high school and postsecondary completion rates, the nation is on track to fall short by up to 3 million postsecondary degrees by 2018.

High school dropouts make an annual average of $19,450, while graduates make an average of $27,380.

High school graduates, on the other hand, provide both economic and social benefits to society. In addition to earning higher wages—resulting in corresponding benefits to local, state, and national economic conditions—high school graduates live longer, are less likely to be teen parents, and are more likely to raise healthier, better-educated children. In fact, children of parents who graduate from high school are far more likely to graduate from high school, compared to children of parents without high school degrees. High school graduates are also less likely to commit crimes, rely on government health care, or use other public services such as food stamps or housing assistance. Additionally, high school graduates engage in civic activity, including voting and volunteering in their communities, and at higher levels.

Reducing Dropouts by Improving High Schools

To increase the number of students who graduate from high school, the nation's secondary schools must address the reasons why most students drop out. In a recent survey of high school dropouts, respondents indicated that they felt alienated at school and that no one noticed if they failed to show up for class. High school dropouts also complained that school did not reflect real-world challenges. More than half of the respondents said that the major reason for dropping out of high school was that they felt their classes were uninteresting and irrelevant.

Others leave because they are not doing well academically. According to the 2009 National Assessment of Educational Progress in reading, only about 30 percent of entering high school freshmen read proficiently, which generally means that as the material in their textbooks becomes more challenging, they drop even further behind.

The nation can no longer afford to have more than one-quarter of its students leave high school without a diploma. High schools must be improved to give all students the excellent education that will prepare them for college and a career, and to be productive members of society.

FIVE

An Emphasis on Vocational Education Could Reduce Dropout Rates

William C. Symonds, Robert B. Schwartz, and Ronald Ferguson

Vocational education programs, in which students learn a trade and graduate with an employable skill, are the norm for many high school students in Europe. This viewpoint, an excerpt from a report published by the Harvard Graduate School of Education, describes the two most common vocational education systems in northern and central Europe and argues that American students would benefit from such a system. Along with preparing students for the workforce, the authors contend that this educational model makes school more relevant to life, keeping students engaged and less likely to drop out.

If you look at the U.S. secondary education system through a comparative lens, one big difference becomes immediately apparent: most advanced nations place far more emphasis on vocational education than we do. Throughout northern and central Europe especially, vocational education and training is a mainstream system, the pathway helping most young people

William C. Symonds, Robert B. Schwartz, and Ronald Ferguson, Excerpted from "Chapter 3: Lessons From Abroad" *Pathways to Prosperity: Meeting the Challenge of Preparing Young Americans for the 21st Century*, February 2011. Copyright © 2011 Harvard Graduate School of Education. All rights reserved. Excerpted and reproduced by permission. Report issued by the Pathways to Prosperity Project, Harvard Graduate School of Education.

make the transition from adolescence to productive adulthood. In Austria, Denmark, Finland, Germany, the Netherlands, Norway, and Switzerland, after grade 9 or 10 between 40 and 70 percent of young people opt for an educational program that typically combines classroom and workplace learning over the next three years. This culminates in a diploma or certificate, a "qualification," as it's called, with real currency in the labor market. In virtually all of these countries, vocational education also provides a pathway into tertiary education for those who choose to take it.

Two Models of Vocational Education

Upper secondary vocational education (or VET, as it is generally known) varies significantly in structure from country to country, but there are two basic models. The first, usually referred to as apprenticeship or the dual system, has students spend three or four days in paid company-organized training at the workplace, with the other day or two in related academic work in the classroom. Germany has the oldest and best-known apprenticeship system, which offers programs leading to recognized qualifications in about 350 different occupations. Switzerland also has a very highly regarded apprenticeship system. A second group of countries have opted for a model in which vocational education is mostly provided in school-based programs, although they all incorporate at least some work-based learning. These countries typically introduce students to a broad cluster of occupations (e.g. health care or IT [information technology]) before narrowing the focus of training in the third year.

From a U.S. perspective perhaps the most important distinction among these countries is the age at which students are separated into different tracks. Germany and Switzerland have separate middle or lower secondary schools based largely on the school's assessment of a student's academic potential. This is a practice we deplore, and it is no surprise that the students in the bottom track German middle schools fare the least well in the labor market. Finland and Denmark, on the other hand, keep all students in a common, untracked comprehensive school up through grade 9

Secondary vocational education includes apprenticing in a trade, such as meat cutting (shown). The author contends that the US educational system could learn from the European vocational models.

or 10, at which point students and their families, not the school, decide which kind of upper secondary education they will pursue. We believe this model makes much more sense for the U.S. to consider, but it would mean that we would have to be willing to abandon our reliance on the various forms of tracking, subtle as well as overt, that pervade much of our education system through the elementary and middle school years.

High School Graduation with Real Qualifications

Despite their highly unattractive early tracking practices, there is much to learn from the German and Swiss apprenticeship systems. In many ways, they exemplify the new 3 "R's" of much

U.S. secondary school reform: rigor, relevance, and relationships. Thanks to high standards, those who complete a VET program have qualifications roughly equivalent to Americans who have earned a technical degree from a community college. As such, they're prepared for more advanced studies in institutions of higher education, such as polytechnics and universities of applied science. The German federal states, which regulate education, are now working to improve access for such students.

In all of these apprenticeship systems employer organizations play a major role. They take the lead in defining occupational qualifications, providing paid apprenticeships or other work-based learning opportunities and (in collaboration with educators and trade union partners) assessing student performance and awarding certificates. In Germany, for example, they pay about half of the expenses associated with the system, contributing roughly as much as the government. Why are they willing to make such a substantial investment?

Simply put, German employers believe that the best way to get a highly qualified workforce is to invest in the development of young workers, participate directly in their training and socialization at the workplace, and then hire those who have proven themselves to be productive at the end of the apprenticeship period. An added incentive is that apprentices can be hired for less than the standard wage, and terminated easily if they don't work out. As a result, some studies suggest that the work and other benefits contributed by apprentices more than offset the costs to employers. No wonder roughly a quarter of German and Swiss employers participate in the dual system.

Clear Occupational Goals

While there is significant variation among the northern and central European countries in the degree of employer ownership, all are characterized by much clearer linkages between labor market needs and educational programs, all offer programs leading to qualifications in a wide range of occupations (white collar as well as blue collar, high tech as well as trades), and all serve a broad cross-section of students. While they all make special efforts to incorporate at-risk students into their programs, in some cases offering employers special incentives to include such students, employers expect their trainees to have a solid foundation of academic skills and a strong work ethic. Consequently, these programs are not designed to serve those with a history of school failure. Rather, they are designed on the premise that many, perhaps most young people would prefer to learn from late adolescence on in an environment in which work and learning are integrated and in which there is a clear occupational goal in sight. And this approach is paying off in increased attainment rates.

By contrast, look at where the United States is ranked relative to other industrialized nations with regard to school and college completion. . . . We have lost enormous ground over the last 15 years. The problem is that while we have been standing still, other nations have leapfrogged us.

Something to Learn

Why is the United States falling behind? It is hardly an accident that most nations with superior attainment rates offer more diverse, robust pathways to careers and practical-minded postsecondary options than we do in the U.S.

Equally damning are results from the OECD's [Organisation for Economic Co-operation and Development] PISA [Programme for International Student Assessment], which tests a national sample of 15-year-olds across member countries every three years in literacy, mathematics, and science. What differentiates PISA from other such assessments is that it is deliberately designed to see how well students can apply what they have learned in school to novel problems and situations, not simply how well they have mastered the curriculum they have been taught. In this sense PISA is designed to measure the kind of thinking and problem-solving skills that employers tell us are most valuable on the job.

Unfortunately, U.S. performance on the four rounds of PISA over the past decade has been uniformly mediocre. In 2009, U.S. students overall scored little better than the OECD average, and

High School Graduation Rates, 1995 and 2005

Percentage of Graduates to the Population at the Typical Age of Graduation, according to the Organisation for Economic Co-operation and Development (OECD)

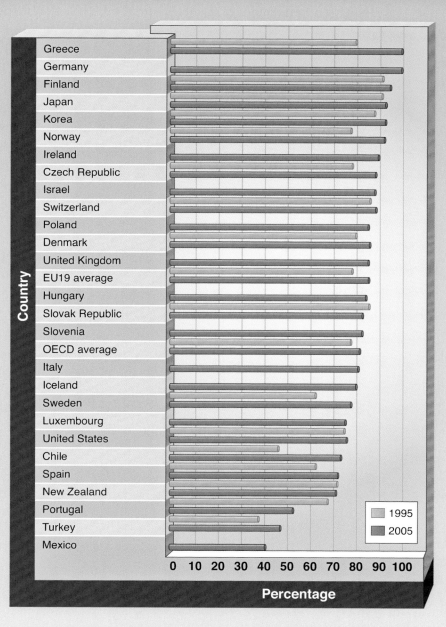

ranked just 17th in science and 25th in math achievement. PISA does more than measure the overall performance of a country's education system in the subjects being assessed. The results can also tell us which countries have the most consistent performance across schools, regardless of demographics, and in which countries such factors as race and socio-economic status have the strongest impact on performance. Again, while the U.S. is not at the bottom of the pack on this criterion, race and poverty play a more significant role in predicting school outcomes here than they do in most other participating countries.

For all these reasons, it is no longer defensible for the U.S. to behave as if it has nothing to learn from other countries. We believe that if the U.S. is serious about increasing the proportion of young people who arrive in their mid-twenties with a post-secondary credential with currency in the labor market, it is imperative that we closely examine the experience of several other OECD countries, especially those with the best developed vocational education systems.

SIX

High-Stakes Testing and Zero-Tolerance Policies Increase Dropout Rates

Advancement Project

> This viewpoint is an excerpt from a report published by the Advancement Project, an organization whose mission it is "to build a fair and just multi-racial democracy using law, public policy, and strategic communications." It explains how standardized testing has become mandatory in schools and argues that what started as merely an effort to make schools and teachers accountable has developed into an incentive for removing troubled and low-performing students from classrooms and even schools, and that zero-tolerance policies have only made it easier to expel "problem" students. Citing statistics, the author also draws a correlation between the implementation of high-stakes testing and the increasing numbers of school dropouts.

While zero-tolerance school discipline and high-stakes testing have each experienced a meteoric rise in recent years, it would be a mistake to view them as being unrelated. . . . These two policies share the same origins and are both products of the same misplaced corporate principles. They are also intimately related in the ways they change the dynamics between schools and the communities they serve. Indeed, zero tolerance and high-stakes testing have become intertwined and even mutually reinforcing, with each helping the other to thrive.

For example, the pressure to improve test scores applied by the No Child Left Behind [NCLB] Act and the high-stakes testing movement makes the public more tolerant of widespread use of zero tolerance and the criminalization of young people by their schools. These policies create the perceived imperative to remove the "bad kids" who prevent the "good kids" from learning. Moreover, there appears to be a direct relationship between the consequences attached to test results and the severity of school disciplinary practices, meaning districts that face the most test pressure will be the most inclined toward punitive measures.

Likewise, zero tolerance becomes the tool used to address the inevitable student backlash from the daily grind of filling in test-booklet bubbles and being subjected to a narrowed, lackluster curriculum. Just as the surest way to avoid student misbehavior is to engage young people with rich course material, perhaps the quickest path toward classroom disruption is to bore students with practice tests and rote memorization exercises. Thus, zero tolerance allows schools under test pressure to quickly remove students who are unwilling or unable to sit quietly in their seats.

A Message That Education Is Not for Everyone

These punitive policies have combined to change the incentive structure for educators, putting many teachers and administrators in the unenviable position of having to choose between their students' interests and their own self-interest. Education has become, more than ever, a "numbers game." The clear message from high-stakes testing policies is that educators' focus should not be on nurturing and educating each child to reach their full potential; their focus should be on getting as many students as possible to reach the level of "proficiency." The message sent by zero-tolerance policies is that education is not for everyone; rather, it is for those students who "deserve" it. The combined

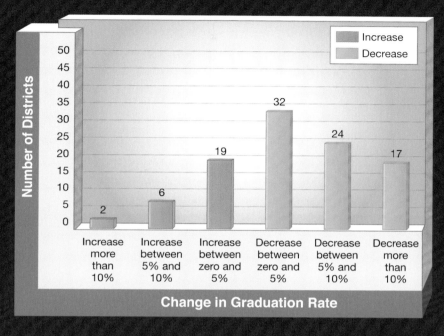

The 100 Largest School Districts: Change in Graduation Rate, 2002 to 2006

effect is that, within this new system of incentives, individual students matter little.

Because of the focus on test scores and the severe consequences attached to them, if a student acts up in class, it is no longer in educators' self-interest to address it by assessing the student's unmet needs or treating the incident as a "teachable moment." Within this business model, it is much easier and more "efficient" to simply remove the child from class through punitive disciplinary measures and focus on the remaining students. With so much riding on these tests, being able to transmit as much of the test material as possible often overrides concerns about the impact such practices have on students.

Pushing Students Out

As a result, the practice of pushing struggling students out of school to boost test scores has become quite common. There are a number of widely used strategies for manipulating test scores, such as withdrawing students from attendance rolls, assigning students to alternative schools, coercing or encouraging students to drop out or enroll in General Educational Development (GED) programs, along with using suspensions, expulsions, and referrals to

The No Child Left Behind Act has come under criticism because of its overemphasis on standardized test scores. Many feel schools are pushing struggling students out of school in order to raise school test scores.

alternative schools. These practices are contemptible, but not surprising when one considers that those educators' future employment or salary may be determined by the results of a single test.

The upshot is that because of zero tolerance and high-stakes testing policies, there is simply no academic safety net for many students. Instead, the existing incentive structure encourages educators to allow huge numbers of students to fall through the cracks of the school system.

The Many Roads to Student Pushout

The combined effect of these dynamics is that countless students are entering the "school-to-prison pipeline" every day. The criminalization of youthful actions in school . . . represents a direct linkage between schools and prisons. But there are also indirect linkages, caused by zero tolerance and high-stakes testing driving students to drop out of school, at which point they become more than eight times as likely to be incarcerated as high school graduates. This can happen in a variety of ways, such as:

- Students are suspended or expelled and then become more likely to fall into additional trouble and less likely to stay on track academically;
- Students are discouraged and ashamed by their low standardized test scores and act out in school until they are removed through suspension, expulsion, or referral to an alternative school;
- As a result of their standardized test scores, students are retained in grade, making them more likely to drop out;
- Students are simply bored by the test-driven curricula and disrupt class, leading to removal from school through punitive discipline; and
- Students are denied a diploma because of a high school exit exam.

Through a variety of means, the get-tough approaches to discipline and accountability can put students on a path toward academic failure that is often difficult to interrupt and has devastating long-term consequences.

The National Picture

Beyond the undeniably negative impact of zero tolerance and high-stakes testing policies on individual students, families, and schools, evidence of more widespread systemic effects is accumulating rapidly. For example, recently-released data show that the nation's graduation rate in 2006—69%—was the lowest it has been since before NCLB was passed. Of particular concern is that the rates for Black and Latino students—51% and 55%, respectively—dropped significantly from 2005 to 2006. Additionally, in 2008, the number of persons taking the GED test was at its highest level since before NCLB. These are all strong indicators of a rampant student pushout problem.

Focusing just on the 100 largest school districts in the country (for which there is now comparable graduation rate data for 1996 through 2006) provides an even better sense of the devastating effects recent policies have had on many communities. These large, mostly urban districts together serve about 40% of the nation's Black, Latino, and Native American students. While graduation rates in most of these districts were improving up until NCLB was signed into law, since then they have deteriorated.

From 1996 until 2002 (when NCLB was signed into law), sixty-eight of the 100 districts experienced rising graduation rates. Twenty-four of those districts achieved double-digit increases in their graduation rates, while only four had double-digit drops during that period.

From that point on, however, the trends have been in the opposite direction. From 2002 until 2006, seventy-three of the 100 largest districts experienced declining graduation rates. Seventeen of those districts experienced at least a double-digit drop in their graduation rates. Only two districts experienced a double-digit increase.

Not only are these districts trending in the wrong direction, their overall graduation rates are now shamefully low. Only 10 of those 100 districts graduated even 80% of their students in 2006. Sixty-seven out of 100 failed to graduate two-thirds of their students, and twenty-five of the districts graduated less than half of their students. Thus, the national disgrace represented by these dismal graduation rates has gotten progressively worse during the NCLB years.

While these developments cannot be solely attributed to zero tolerance and high-stakes testing, the impact of "get-tough" policies do become apparent when examining individual states. There is a familiar pattern that has developed in many states in recent years: first, the implementation of greater "accountability" in the form of high-stakes tests; followed by dramatic increases in the use of zero-tolerance school discipline; then the appearance of "collateral damage" such as more students being enrolled in special education programs, more students being retained in grade, more high school dropouts taking the GED exam, and declining teacher morale; and finally, the pushout of huge numbers of students, exemplified by plummeting or abysmally low graduation rates.

SEVEN

Separate Schools for Minorities Are Not the Answer to the Dropout Crisis

Jan Wong

To address the school dropout crisis, educators, parents, and community members have employed the creation of separate schools for minorities. Jan Wong, a columnist for *Toronto Life*, argues against the idea, stating that it is no different than the segregation struck down in the 1950s. Further, she contends that little research supports the practice and that public schools open to everyone help people understand each other. She also discusses the difficult and painful experiences her grandparents faced upon their immigration to Canada and how she believes people need to look at the present and the future and move beyond the past.

The tall black man was angry. "I want to propose 10 seconds of silence in memory of [Canadian civil rights activist] Brother Dudley Laws," he said into the microphone, his voice booming through the auditorium at Oakwood Collegiate. It was question period at a raucous, emotionally raw public meeting in

March [2011], called after news leaked that the Toronto [Ontario] District School Board [TDSB] had recommended embedding the city's first Africentric high school inside Oakwood. Parents, students, teachers, alumni and neighbours had filled every creaky, green-leatherette flip-up seat.

Laws, the civil rights activist, had died the week before. The man hoping to commemorate him applauded his own suggestion, smacking hands the size of baseball mitts together, before returning to his seat. I half hoped that Karen Falconer, the school board superintendent who was chairing the meeting, would ride him out of order. But Falconer immediately rose to her feet and announced a moment of silence.

Twenty-First-Century Segregation

It was like a scene from the American pre–civil rights era of the 1950s and '60s, except that this time the tables were turned: angry blacks demanding segregation before a shell-shocked mixed-race community, while uniformed cops kept wary watch.

Civil rights redux? Or civil wrongs? Subdividing schools into silos is the TDSB's latest strategy for fixing chronic underachievement among specific racial and ethnic groups. At the Oakwood meeting, Jim Spyropoulos, the board's superintendent of inclusive schools (a position created last spring), rattled off the list. "I'm going to name the groups that are underachieving: blacks, specifically of Caribbean origin; Aboriginals; Portuguese; Latinos; Middle Eastern."

The idea is that students who are failing can build self-esteem, become more engaged and ultimately succeed if they're surrounded by others like themselves. Toronto already has two segregated elementary schools, one for blacks and one for Aboriginals [native peoples]. Now two new high schools are under consideration: one for black students (proposed at Oakwood), nearly 40 per cent of whom don't graduate; and one for Portuguese students, who have a 38 per cent dropout rate. The Portuguese school proposal is in its very early stages, one of several options being considered by a new TDSB task force that's expected to deliver its recommendations later this year [2011].

Research Is Lacking

Research on the success of segregated learning is scarce. The TDSB, while considering Toronto's first Africentric school (now embedded in Sheppard Public School in North York), looked at the effectiveness of black-focused schools in the United States and found little in the way of comparative data. Even where there is data, it's impossible to account for differences in class, culture or home environment. The TDSB report concluded there were few studies that clearly demonstrated the effectiveness of Africentric schools or programs.

Toronto, Ontario, has created minority schools to address the dropout crisis. Critics argue, however, that plan is equal to segregation.

In the absence of solid research—and desperate to remedy the problem—the TDSB forged ahead anyway, framing the move toward segregated learning as an attempt to give parents more choice. But compartmentalization won't address the main cause of educational disaffection among marginalized students—specifically, an inequitable and inflexibly funded system that's already divided into have and have-not schools.

A Failed Experiment

Toronto's First Nations School (at Dundas and Broadview) has been operating for 34 years and runs from junior kindergarten through Grade 8. It was created to provide, tradition-based learning for children of Anishinaabe descent; teachers give out feathers for achievement in academics, behaviour, attendance and participation. Today, the school's 92 kids serve as an example of what can happen to a vulnerable student population that is isolated and, it would seem, largely forgotten.

In the most recent test results available, for 2008–10, 92 per cent of third graders failed to meet the [Ontario] provincial standard for reading and math. Eighty per cent were below the standard in writing. Sixth graders tested even more poorly. A stunning 100 per cent were below the provincial standard in math, 93 per cent in reading and 87 per cent in writing. Many of the students have learning disabilities, which may explain the low test scores. Clearly, segregating them has not solved their problems. The school has posted such horrific results, it's bordering on criminal that it hasn't been shut down.

At the Africentric elementary school, which opened two years ago, the kids sing two anthems during morning assembly: "O Canada" and the African-American national anthem, "Lift Every Voice and Sing." Teachers offer an African take on everything from reading to math: when kindergarteners learn the principles of geometric shapes, for instance, their teacher shows them the corresponding shapes on an African Ndebele hut. Never mind that such cultural symbols may hold little significance for a child of, say, third-generation Jamaican-Canadians.

The school didn't have a Grade 6 at the time of the last testing period, so the only measurements available are for its third graders. These are terrific: 81 per cent of its students are at or above the provincial standard in both writing and math; 69 per cent are at or above that standard in reading. The results are encouraging, but also what you might expect from a new school with small class sizes (the inaugural third grade class had only 16 children) and from students with obviously engaged parents (the very act of "choosing" the school is a good indication that they are more involved in their child's education).

A Misguided Idea

I'm not against specialized curricula, but having separate schools for blacks or other ethnic students is as offensive as white-only washrooms. I object to educational apartheid because it turns back the clock on civil rights. Nearly a century ago, my late aunt Ming broke through the colour barrier in Victoria, B.C. [British Columbia]. Family lore has it that on her first day of school, she took one look at the dingy classrooms in Chinatown and marched over to the school for white children. Miraculously and mysteriously, they enrolled her, and she went on to graduate from the University of Toronto as one of Canada's first female Chinese anesthetists.

Schools socialize us into becoming Canadians. They help us cross class and racial lines so we can head into the workplace. Separate schools with monocultural learning environments are antithetical to the principles on which our public school system is based: openness, integration, cohesion. How can you eliminate racism by segregating along racial lines?

At Oakwood that night, Kativa Turner, a 17-year-old student at Malvern Collegiate, was one of the audience members who spoke. "You guys don't understand my pain," she said, before explaining that she had waited her "whole life" for an Africentric high school. Alternately tearful and spitting mad, she added, "Turner is not my name. That's the name of my slave owner. Nobody ever thinks of *that*."

Sense of Belonging Among Immigrants to Canada and Their Children

Visible minorities (those with dark skin) are less likely to feel accepted in Canadian society than white immigrants, and second-generation immigrants are less likely to feel accepted than their parents, according to a study in which 41,666 people were interviewed in nine languages. The study found that skin color was the biggest hurdle to feelings of belonging, a more important factor than that of either religion or income.

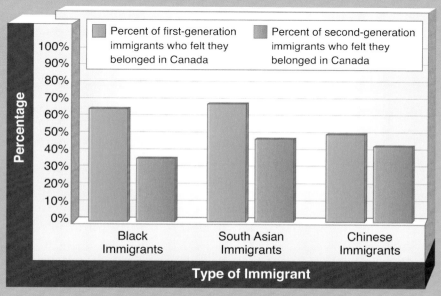

Taken from: Lesley Ciarula Taylor. "Darker the Skin, Less You Fit," February 18, 2012. www.thestar.com.

When my grandfather came to B.C. as a coolie [Asian slave or manual laborer] in 1880, the government bureaucrat who processed his entry anglicized his Chinese name as "Hooie." Imagine his pain. Which was nothing, of course, compared to enduring the anti-Chinese riots in the province in 1907. But there's no point in competing over personal histories. Everyone has one, and some are sadder than others. Our problem isn't the past. It's the present, and our future.

EIGHT

New Strategies by Educators Are Decreasing Minority Dropout Rates

Ed Finkel

The educational achievement gap between African American students and their white counterparts has been the topic of intense study. Black students are more likely to score lower on standardized tests, to be suspended or expelled, and to drop out of school. Ed Finkel, an independent writer specializing in education, community development, and youth, writes here for *District Administration*, a monthly newsmagazine targeted at school district decision makers. Finkel explains the achievement gap and highlights successful attempts by some school districts working to close it: a "youth ambassador" program in Baltimore, Maryland; a partnership project with the court system in Birmingham, Alabama; and charter schools in Harlem, New York.

It's a familiar refrain in American education: African-American children score lower on standardized tests, graduate high school at lower rates, and are considerably more likely to be suspended or expelled than the general population. Two recent reports, one from the Council of the Great City Schools and one from the

American Institutes for Research, reveal that the achievement gaps are still large between African-American and white students.

But concerted efforts in certain states and districts have shown that the historical trend doesn't have to remain the same, and overall the picture may have brightened slightly over the past decade or two, according to statistics and anecdotal observations.

Still, some activist groups and educational researchers fear the systematic federal evaluations conducted under the No Child Left Behind law have given districts and states powerful incentives to move lower-achieving students out of their general populations to special education placements, alternative schools, or elsewhere—perhaps dovetailing with an urgency to create zero-tolerance discipline policies.

A report from the Washington [D.C.]-based Advancement Project, called "Test, Punish and Push Out," makes a stark accusation: "The practice of pushing struggling students out of school to boost test scores has become quite common."

The report, released last January [2010] focuses on graduation rates in the nation's 25 largest school districts with at least 80 percent black and Latino student enrollment, in the years immediately before and after No Child Left Behind was passed. From 1996 to 2002, 19 of these 25 districts saw graduation rates increase, 11 of them by more than 10 percent. But after the law passed, from 2002 to 2006, 19 of the 25 saw graduation rates decrease, eight by more than 10 percent.

A Disturbing Correlation

Those figures support the theory that the pressure to boost test scores after No Child Left Behind led students to be pushed out, although Jim Freeman, project director with Advancement Project's Ending the Schoolhouse to Jailhouse Track project, acknowledges the numbers do not provide hard proof. "It's correlation evidence but not causation evidence," he says. "We're trying to get behind those numbers and figure out what's going on. Policies like exclusionary discipline, and high-stakes testing and tracking, have created a hostile and alienating environment, particularly for students of color."

Horace Hall, education professor at DePaul University and a former special education teacher in Chicago Public Schools [in Illinois], sees a different connection between achievement and discipline: black students, particularly boys, being erroneously shunted to special ed because they're behind in reading, then developing behavior disorders due to mislabeling.

"If you're behind two or three years in reading because you weren't taught the basics by third grade, [and] you're supposed to be an independent reader—[then] you're labeled as learning disabled," he says. "You're told you're a dummy. You get angry about that. And then you've been labeled a behavior disorder."

Freeman cites as a model the Baltimore City Public Schools [in Maryland], which has a student body that's 88 percent African-American. A reworking and rethinking of the district's get-tough disciplinary policies focusing more on prevention and intervention techniques rather than punitive measures have led to a drop in out-of-school suspensions from 16,752 to 9,705 in the last three years, says Jonathan Brice, the district's executive director of student support. And less punitive discipline can help catalyze academic growth in part because students are not out of school serving suspensions and they're not potentially getting messages that school is not the place for them. Dropout rates fell 34 percent between 2006–2007 and 2008–2009, district figures show, while standardized test scores rose across all grade levels.

"As our suspension numbers have gone down, we've seen achievement go up, and our attendance has improved as well," Brice says. "They're all interrelated. They're all interwoven. You can't look at one in isolation. What you realize is that our focus has to be on young people coming into an environment where they're able to learn. You've got to set the conditions that will allow that to occur." . . .

Blacks Still Punished

Federal statistics on suspensions and expulsions lend credence to the claim that African-American students are punished dispro-

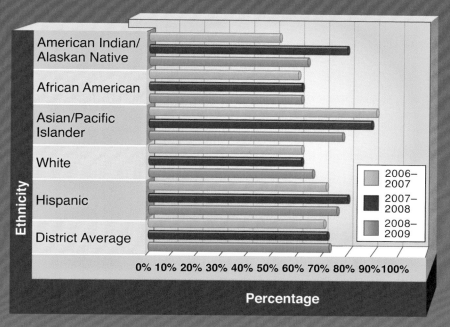

Graduation Rates of Baltimore City Public Schools, 2006–2009

Ethnicity (vertical axis)

- American Indian/Alaskan Native
- African American
- Asian/Pacific Islander
- White
- Hispanic
- District Average

Legend:
- 2006–2007
- 2007–2008
- 2008–2009

0% 10% 20% 30% 40% 50% 60% 70% 80% 90% 100%

Percentage

portionately. Out of the 48.5 million total students in the 2006 DOE [US Department of Education] Office of Civil Rights report, 17 percent were African-American, but blacks were more than double the percentage of those impacted by corporal punishment (36 percent), out-of-school suspension (37 percent) and expulsions (38 percent).

A recent study from the Southern Poverty Law Center, which draws upon four decades of federal data on 9,220 of the country's 16,000 public middle schools, reveals that black boys were three times as likely to be suspended as white boys, and black girls were four times as likely to be suspended as white girls. The study, "Suspended Education: Urban Middle Schools in Crisis," showed increases in suspension rates overall and for black students. Between 1973 and 2006, the figure climbed from 4 percent to 7 percent of all students, and from 6 percent to 15 percent of all black students.

"The suspensions and expulsions are out of control in a lot of our high schools," [senior policy associate at the Children's

A report on graduation rates in the nation's twenty-five largest school districts with at least 80 percent black and Latino students found that between 2002 and 2006, nineteen of the twenty-five saw graduation rates increase.

Defense Fund Gill] Cook says. "It's pushing a lot of kids into juvenile justice, directly, or pushing them out into the streets. When children are suspended for 35 and 45 days, you can't make up that year of school—ever. It's creating dropouts. And it's often for very arbitrary reasons—three strikes and you're out—or just being late to school."

Freeman agrees that strict zero-tolerance discipline often leads to many students falling below grade-level testing targets, which is also prevalent in drop-out factories. "These places that have very high suspension and expulsion rates, and excessive reliance on law enforcement—those are the students who are creating the achievement gap," he says. "We're talking about two weeks or a month out of class."

Baltimore's Youth Ambassadors

Advancement Project has been working closely with Baltimore City Public Schools, where Freeman says CEO Andres Alonso has "taken school discipline issues very seriously. They've been focusing more on prevention and intervention techniques rather than punitive measures," he says.

Brice says the district three years ago overhauled its code of conduct, saving out-of-school suspensions for the most egregious offenses while attempting to return kids to the straight-and-narrow through a "comprehensive and robust level of support for students" that includes an IEP [individualized education program]-like team of psychologists, social workers and administrators that's deployed whenever a student's behavior and/or academic record raises red flags. "It's the code of conduct. It's the support for kids, so kids aren't acting up. It's the early identification," Brice says. "When you put all those things in place, kids respond, parents respond. You change the culture from one in which it's about putting kids out on the street, to one in which it's about helping young people be successful."

Chief Academic Officer Sonja Santelises adds that the district has worked to identify students who have leadership potential but seem in danger of using those skills to the wrong ends, such as on behalf of street gangs, and has encouraged them to join a leadership development program called "youth ambassadors." These ambassadors become a sounding board for other students and a "student cabinet" of sorts that speaks with the principal about concerns.

Although such initiatives don't specifically target African-Americans, Santelises says they might be the most [benefited]. "It is important for young African-American students to know they can lead . . . because they live in a culture where, our current president notwithstanding, they don't get that message," she says.

The district tries to instill a message about the importance of achievement. "How do we support kids to build the skills for resilience when many of them live in environments where it is a major feat to get up and come to school in the morning?" she asks.

Birmingham Redeemed

Freeman also favorably cites Birmingham (Ala.) City Schools as a district that's created a partnership with the local court system to ensure that while schools are kept safe, students whose disciplinary infractions are first-time and nonviolent receive a lesser consequence, such as community service, so they can stay in school and, when possible, avoid a criminal record.

Superintendent Craig Witherspoon says his district is coupling that with beefed-up curriculum rigor—from a wider array of Advanced Placement classes, to a middle-school program called "Laying the Foundation" that prepares students for such classes—and more professional development and formative assessments.

"We know that African-American students, whether in poverty or nonpoverty, can achieve at a higher level," says Witherspoon, whose district is more than 98 percent black and has seen graduation rates fluctuate between 80 percent and 86 percent over the past six years. The graduation rate is often affected by issues in elementary and middle school. "We're attempting to identify students a lot earlier and look at what structures we have in place to support them," he says.

Witherspoon says that for children from troubled backgrounds, that can mean partnering with social service agencies. "If their home life is such that school is not a priority, . . . you have to make sure those supports are in place," he says.

Charter School Charm

Among the organizations often cited by educational experts as displaying best practices in lifting up poor and minority children is the Harlem Children's Zone in New York, which runs two charter schools and after-school programming that provides the kind of wraparound services that Witherspoon mentions.

The charter schools, which feature longer days and school years than most public schools, are too new to have NAEP [National Assessment of Educational Progress] data to prove their success, says Marty Lipp, spokesman for Harlem Children's Zone. But among those participating in the after-school programs, where they receive homework help, tutoring, health care and social work interventions as needed, 90 percent have not only graduated high school but have gone to college. Suspension and expulsion rates are "negligible," Lipp says, adding that most students in the charter schools and after-school programs are black and Latino.

"We do whatever it takes," Lipp says. "Whatever the barrier is to learning, we try to erase. . . . It's a broader definition of education, [and] in a sense [it's] going into youth development."

NINE

The Dropout Crisis Is Also Rural

Mary Ann Zehr

The high school dropout crisis has largely been reported as concentrated in urban areas with very large school districts; however, rural areas, many with small districts and small classroom sizes, are also facing troubles. In fact, one-fifth of the schools labeled as "dropout factories" are in rural districts. Mary Ann Zehr, an assistant editor at *Education Week*, documents this underreported issue, explaining the extent of the problem, including why so many teens in rural areas drop out, what their lives look like, and what rural schools are doing to encourage students to be more successful in school and to graduate with their classes.

In the foothills of the Appalachian Mountains here in the northwest corner of South Carolina, high schools' attempts to curb student dropouts may not match what many people picture when they hear talk of the nation's "dropout factories." Yet one-fifth of the 2,000 high schools nationwide categorized that way by researchers at Johns Hopkins University are in rural areas, some of them small schools where students get a lot of personal attention.

Mary Ann Zehr, "Rural 'Dropout Factories' Often Overshadowed: Some High Schools Are Fighting the Odds by Employing Research-Based Strategies," *Education Week*, v. 29, no. 27, March 31, 2010, pp. 1–3. Copyright © 2010 by Editorial Projects in Education. All rights reserved. Reproduced by permission of Editorial Projects in Education.

With 50 such schools, South Carolina tops all other states in the number of rural schools on the dropout-factory list, with Georgia and North Carolina not far behind. Nearly half of those South Carolina schools have fewer than 500 students.

The Example of Oconee County

Tamassee-Salem Middle and High School here in Oconee County is among them. It has 154 students in grades 9–12 and is located in a town with fewer than 150 people whose commercial area consists of a convenience store, a dollar store, three churches, and a gas station. The school's challenge of graduating students illustrates that it's no simple endeavor to help them see the relevance of an education. "We have generational poverty, a lack of aspirations," said Michael Lucas, the superintendent of the 10,400-student Oconee County school district.

Besides Tamassee-Salem, the county's West-Oak Senior High School, which enrolls about 1,000 students, is also on the rural dropout-factory list. The district's two other high schools are rural but didn't make the cutoff point for the list. The lion's share of students in all four schools are white, many of them poor. Mr. Lucas said the parents and grandparents of some children in Oconee County didn't finish high school so many of the current crop of students think, "Why should I?"

Despite such sentiments, the district is working to ensure that children read by 3rd grade to help them be successful over the long term, he said. The district also spent federal economic-stimulus aid this school year [2009–2010] on hiring "adequate-yearly-progress coaches" who monitor struggling students and track them down if they miss school. If students fail a class, they can make it up online as part of a credit-recovery program.

In an area with a lot of youths who prefer to work with their hands rather than read books, the county has strong career and technical institutions. The district also runs an alternative school, charged with helping students at risk of dropping out get back on track.

The 2004 report "Locating the Dropout Crisis" first drew attention to a list of about 2,000 high schools that researchers

South Carolina tops all states in the number of rural schools on the "dropout-factory" list.

considered to be dropout factories—"an institution that does a good job of systematically producing dropouts," said Thomas C. West, a University of Chicago researcher who is affiliated with the Everyone Graduates Center at Johns Hopkins University, which put out the report.

Since the inception of the list, most of the attention to the nation's dropout problem has been on urban schools, where the average graduation rate for the class of 2006 was 58.7 percent, compared with 73.1 percent in rural schools, according to *Diplomas Count 2009*.

Mr. West says the high number of rural dropout factories in South Carolina, likely results from the lack of jobs and persistent poverty. Still, he sees an advantage to working on the dropout crisis in rural vs. urban areas: Schools have fewer students, and "you can put more emphasis on what's going on in their lives."

Different Measures

Historically, the inhabitants of Tamassee and Salem could drop out of high school and get jobs in textile mills. But those mills have closed, and the region's manufacturers of electronic components, fiberglass insulation, and the like want students to earn at least a high school diploma or General Educational Development— GED—certificate, educators here say.

Steve M.R. Moore, the principal of Tamassee-Salem, is not happy with his school's rate for students graduating in four years, which was 75 percent in 2009. But he implores people to understand what is behind the statistic and to acknowledge steps he and his staff members are taking to increase the rate. They've seen some success: In 2007, the rate was 66.7 percent.

"The key is about building relationships and making sure the students can see they can be successful," Mr. Moore said.

While the Johns Hopkins researchers have highlighted a problem at Tamassee-Salem, others have lauded the school's accomplishments. In 2007, U.S. News & World Report gave it a bronze award for being one of South Carolina's best high schools. In 2008, the school was one of 25 in the South to receive a Pacesetter award from the High Schools That Work initiative of the Southern Regional Education Board.

"Unfortunately, people take the dropout-factory label as a stigmatizing term rather than a helpful term," said Mr. West, noting that the point of the label is to get policymakers to focus on the problem. "Some schools need total reform; some may just need a lot of help. Some are doing well, but a couple of kids [in them] need extra help," he said. Actually, the dropout-factory classification isn't based on schools' official dropout rates. At both Tamassee-Salem and West-Oak, the rate reported to the state in 2008 was 5.4 percent.

Mr. West and Robert Balfanz, the co-director of the Everyone Graduates Center, put a school on the dropout-factory list when, on average over three school years, the number of seniors is 60 percent or less than the number of freshmen at that school three years earlier.

By contrast, the graduation rate that schools report to South Carolina officials according to federal guidelines is the percentage of 9th graders at a school who earn regular high school diplomas and graduate in four years or less. It also includes students who enrolled in 9th grade for the first time elsewhere and then transferred to that school. Special education students who get certificates rather than high school diplomas count against the graduation rate. So do students who left school and then got a GED certificate, or who took more than four years to earn a diploma.

The dropout rate reported to the state applies to a single school year. It refers to students who leave school during that year and don't transfer to another school.

Future Paths

It's possible to find dropouts in the district's adult education program in Seneca trying to get a GED. One of them is Allen R. Ellis, 17, who attended both West-Oak and Tamassee-Salem high schools. He was expelled from West-Oak Senior High. Later, he attended Tamassee-Salem High but dropped out after a couple of weeks because, he said, the school didn't recognize how smart he was and told him he'd be able to get only a certificate, not a regular diploma. Because of his lack of high school credits, Mr. Ellis said, it would have taken him until he was 21 to get a diploma, which he found discouraging. He said he had often moved from school to school because his father was in the military and had failed classes because he didn't do his homework. With a GED, he said, "I can join the military or go to college a whole lot sooner." He now works part time in construction.

Another young adult working on a GED, Holly Galbreath, 19, says she doesn't think administrators and teachers at West-Oak, where she dropped out halfway through her junior year, could have done much to keep her in school. "I got in with the wrong crowd," she said. "I started caring more about myself and my having a good time than my education."

In middle school, she said, she was motivated to keep at least a C average, in order to participate in extracurricular activities, such as cheerleading. But in 10th grade, she said, she dropped extracurricular activities, skipped school, and did drugs. "I was so far behind that it was going to be impossible to catch up," she said. But Ms. Galbreath said she now wants to go to college so she can work in a field she enjoys, such as photography. She doesn't want to work in a factory.

Right now, the adult education program has 59 students who are ages 17 to 19. Steve Willis, its director, said the program serves about 130 students in that age bracket and gives out about 75 GED certificates and 10 high school diplomas to that group each year.

Matt Hunter is not among them. A dropout from West-Oak, he's not working on a GED and doesn't expect to return to the classroom. The 22-year-old lives with his girlfriend at his grandparents' house in Westminster. He's worked in landscaping before, and from time to time his neighbor pays him cash for helping him repair cars.

His girlfriend, Hali Cannon, 18, graduated from Seneca High School, also in Oconee County, and recently brought in some money working at a doughnut shop. "I've been happy lately," Mr. Hunter said. "Every time we need money, it pops up."

Mr. Hunter said he liked math and Junior Reserve Officers' Training Corps because the teachers of that class had a sense of humor. But he disliked English class. Back in 5th grade, he had been diagnosed with dyslexia and repeated that grade. While he can read if he has to, he avoids it. As a 10th grader, he was badly injured when a car hit him while he rode a bike. He had to get around West-Oak in a wheelchair, which was difficult. "Mom said if I wanted to quit, I could," he said, and he did.

"Whatever It Takes"

Tamassee-Salem High has a slogan this year of "whatever it takes," which Candice Brucke, the assistant principal, said means the school's educators aim to do whatever it takes to ensure each student gets a diploma. Tamassee-Salem, she noted, is already implementing the six dropout-prevention strategies recommended in a practice guide published by the U.S. Department of Education's Institute of Education Sciences. One of those strategies is assigning advocates to at-risk students. The school is in its third year of running a program

Reading Scores: Fourth Grade Boys, 2009 National Assessment of Educational Progress

As these percentages indicate, the educational crisis in the United States is not limited to large cities.

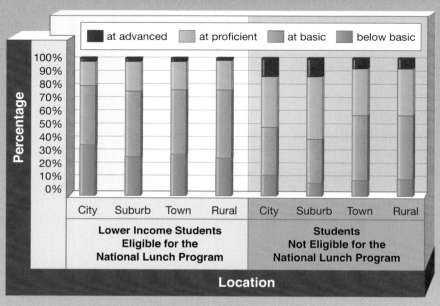

Taken from: US Department of Education.

Baltimore City Public Schools' Graduation Rates from 2006–2007 to 2008–2009

Graduation Rates						
Year	American Indian Alaskan Native	African American	Asian/ Pacific Islander	Whites	Hispanic	District Average
SY 2006–07	53.33	59.69	90.63	61.93	71.15	60.05
SY 2007–08	78.57	62.24	88.37	62.02	79.49	62.65
SY 2008–09	65.00	62.22	77.14	66.20	75.34	62.69

Taken from: Baltimore City Public Schools.

in which well-educated retirees from an affluent community nearby mentor students one on one. Jane Brosnan, a retired software engineer who designed the program with the principal, said she believes that by providing a listening ear and encouragement, the mentors have helped some students pass their classes.

Tyler Galloway, a student at Tamassee-Salem, thought about leaving school because "I just get bored." Principal Moore talked with him about sticking it out, he said, and he thinks he will "because I'm so close now." A junior, Mr. Galloway has passed the state's high school exit exam and is on track with his classes. He said he's had some unexcused absences and plans to make them up, a state requirement.

The 17-year-old said the chance to take welding courses at Hamilton Career Center, the district's career and technical school, has also helped him stay in school. His goal is to get a welding job at Duke Energy, which runs a nuclear-power plant close to Salem.

Mr. Moore said that in his eight years as principal, he's tried to improve the quality of education at his school. Though the school is too small to offer Advanced Placement classes, he said, students can take such courses at other high schools in the county. Last year, he said, one student took advantage of that option. This year, no one has. He's pushed for 8th graders to take algebra, and the school is now offering calculus for the first time in a decade.

An audit last year by a High Schools That Work team found many promising practices at the school. For instance, it had implemented up-to-date technology and ensured that all teachers are certified. The team, however, said it saw a lack of consistency in the use of innovative teaching strategies to engage students.

Maureese Robinson, the director of academic assistance at Tamassee-Salem for middle and high schoolers, works from lists of students who have failed classes or haven't passed the state's exit exam to identify those who need extra help. He runs an after-school homework center and Saturday school and stays in touch by phone with parents of struggling students. "Whether they dropped out or not [themselves], I don't think any parent wants their kid to drop out of school," Mr. Robinson said. "I can't see that in any town. Some have more control over their kids than others."

Decreasing the Dropout Rate Requires Multiple Solutions

Dale Mezzacappa

Philadelphia, Pennsylvania, is one of the cities where the high school graduation rate has reached crisis proportions; in 2001 less than 50 percent of students entering ninth grade graduated four years later. In the past few years, however, Philadelphia, unlike most major cities, has seen a significant decrease in the dropout rate. Dale Mezzacappa, a former reporter for the *Philadelphia Inquirer* and a contributing editor of the independent *Philadelphia Public School Notebook*, writing here for the *Washington Monthly*, highlights the long history of Philadelphia's educational reform efforts and describes the more recent efforts that seem to be making the most difference.

No major city in America has worked longer and harder on its dropout problem than Philadelphia. Yet those efforts, going back nearly half a century, have gained traction only in the last ten years. Between 2001 and 2009 the percentage of Philadelphia students who entered ninth grade and graduated in four years increased from 48 percent to 56 percent. Those gains might seem modest, and are clearly insufficient. But the fact that they occurred at all, and at a time when dropout rates

Dale Mezzacappa, "Philadelphia: After Decades of Effort, a Decade of Progress," *The Washington Monthly*, July/August 2010, pp. A10-A12. Copyright © 2010 by Washington Monthly Publishing, LLC, 733 15th St. NW, Suite 520, Washington DC 20005. (202) 393-5155. Website: www.washingtonmonthly.com. All rights reserved. Reproduced by permission.

nationally have not budged, suggests that Philadelphia is doing something right.

It's a measure of the complexity of the problem, however, that it is difficult to discern which of the flurry of policies and practices that have been tried here are responsible for the gains. Unlike in New York, Philadelphia has not followed a single blueprint or plan. Instead, the work on the issue has accreted over time, with new reforms and initiatives, most of them privately conceived or supported, added to the mix along the way. In the last five years [2005–2010] the city has concentrated on providing students with an ever-growing array of options to the city's traditional high schools—charter schools, small alternative or "accelerated" schools—based on students' needs and inclination. Yet some of the most promising experiments in reform have also occurred in the city's traditional high schools, which the vast majority of its students still attend. But for bureaucratic and budgetary reasons those initiatives have seldom been sustained. If Philadelphia wants to continue to make progress, it'll have to find a way to do so, and the [Barack] Obama administration's efforts to combat the dropout problem could provide some real help.

A Demand for Better Schools

In 1968, Philadelphia's business, political, and civic elite got together to figure out how to get more high school kids to stay in school and prevent them from being swept up in the maelstrom of anger and urban violence touched off by the assassinations of Martin Luther King Jr. and Robert F. Kennedy. The year before, as many as 3,500 African American students demonstrated at school district headquarters demanding better schools, more black teachers, and culturally relevant courses and textbooks.

Career Academies

The big idea the leaders formulated was career academies: subunits within large neighborhood schools that blended academics with a vocational training and established stronger relationships between students and their peers and teachers. The first such academy in the nation, focused on preparing students for jobs in the electrical field, opened in 1969 at Thomas Edison High School, which had the highest dropout rate in the city. New career academies were started throughout the 1970s and '80s, and by the mid-'90s there were twenty-nine in the city and several thousand nationwide. Extensive research deemed the academies to be a successful anti-dropout strategy.

Over the next thirty years, with strong support and substantial nudging from the city's foundations and private sector, the school district would attack the dropout problem in a number of other ways. In 1982, when Constance Clayton became superintendent, she looked at the city's neighborhood high schools and saw "lethargy and sameness and undue stability of faculty and administrators." She said in a 1993 interview that she saw good anti-dropout programs, career academies among them, but they reached only a relatively small number of students in what was then a school district of more than 200,000 students.

Embracing the efforts of the Philadelphia High Schools Collaborative, an outside organization dedicated to reforming city high schools, she decided to shake things up. The Collaborative effort built on the career academies example and divided the high schools into smaller, semi-autonomous units within one building that focused more attention on incoming ninth graders. Good results were seen almost immediately at three pilot schools—better attendance, more success in classes, a more studious atmosphere. Eventually, twenty-two high schools were using parts of the strategy and 20,000 students were being affected. The goal was to create more intimate, personalized environments for learning, a concept that still drives much of the thinking on how to reduce the dropout rate.

Lost Progress

But the kinds of problems that typically squelch major reforms in large urban school districts were present in Philadelphia as well. Skeptics questioned the statistics showing improvement. The Philadelphia teachers union objected to making the smaller

High School Dropout Rate by Sex

The percentage of high school dropouts, ages 16–24, has declined since 1960. The percentage of male students who dropped out of high school has decreased from 27.8% in 1960 to 8.5% in 2008. The percentage of female dropouts has decreased from 26.7% to 7.5%.

Percentage of Dropouts in the United States from 1960 to 2008, Selected Years

Year	Total	Male	Female
1960	27.2%	27.8%	26.7%
1970	15.0%	14.2%	15.7%
1980	14.1%	15.1%	13.1%
1985	12.6%	13.4%	11.8%
1990	12.1%	12.3%	11.8%
1992	11.0%	11.3%	10.7%
1993	11.0%	11.2%	10.9%
1994	11.4%	12.3%	10.6%
1995	12.0%	12.2%	11.7%
1996	11.1%	11.4%	10.9%
1997	11.0%	11.9%	10.1%
1998	11.8%	13.3%	10.3%
1999	11.2%	11.9%	10.5%
2000	10.9%	12.0%	9.9%
2001	10.7%	12.2%	9.3%
2002	10.5%	11.8%	9.2%
2003	9.9%	11.3%	8.4%
2004	10.3%	11.6%	9.0%
2005	9.4%	10.8%	8.0%
2006	9.3%	10.3%	8.3%
2007	8.7%	9.8%	7.7%
2008	8.0%	8.5%	7.5%

Taken from: US Dept. of Education. National Center for Education Statistics, *Digest of Education Statistics 2007*.

units equivalent to separate schools, which affected teachers' seniority and job security. Money problems grew. Clayton also had her differences with the Collaborative; she retired in 1993, and the effort faded. The "small learning communities" continued to exist, but lost the autonomy that made them effective. In many high schools, they began to function like academic tracks, separating students by ability. Meanwhile, vocational career academies were reduced in number, from twenty-nine in the '90s to only ten today.

It's impossible to say what effect these on-again-off-again reforms had on the school district's overall dropout rate. By narrowly defining who was a dropout, Philadelphia and other school districts had for decades been underreporting their actual attrition rates. Whatever the effect of the anti-dropout measures, they were overwhelmed by the flight of white and black working and middle-class families to the suburbs and a growing poverty rate in the city, which rose from 15 percent in 1970 to 24 percent today, according to U.S. Census data. Students were promoted in elementary and middle schools even though they weren't learning fundamental skills; by 2000 more than 75 percent of the students who enrolled in the district's neighborhood high schools were far behind academically.

Talent Development High Schools

In 1999, Philadelphia's civic community pushed yet another remedy aimed at reworking the high schools that Clayton, more than a decade before, had characterized as outmoded and resistant to change. The Philadelphia Education Fund, which combines money from foundations, wealthy individuals, corporations, and public agencies, persuaded the school district to bring in a new approach to its worst schools. The model, developed at Johns Hopkins University, was called Talent Development High Schools, and its primary goal was to keep ninth graders on track toward graduation by making sure they passed all of their courses. Over the next four years, the model would show progress in seven of the district's high schools. A 2004 evaluation by MDRC, the public policy research organization, found that the Talent Development schools "produced substantial gains in academic course credits earned and promotion rates and modest improvements in attendance."

In 2002, Paul Vallas, the energetic, do-it-all-at-once former CEO of the Chicago Public Schools, was hired as Philadelphia's sixth superintendent in thirty years. He arrived just after the state had declared the Philadelphia schools financially and academically bankrupt, replaced the mayorally appointed school board with a School Reform Commission with a majority named by the governor, and demanded that the district turn over many of its worst-performing schools to private, sometimes for-profit operators. Vallas embraced the "diverse provider" strategy even as he continued to push for more money and implement his own agenda. After the MDRC study came out, Vallas said the district could not afford to continue the existing Talent Development High Schools, let alone expand the program intact. Instead, he said all the neighborhood schools would borrow some ideas from Talent Development.

James Kemple, the researcher who headed up the study of Talent Development, was at the meeting in which Vallas said he'd do his own take on the model. Kemple cautioned him against trying to do it piecemeal. "I was trying to make the case with Paul that the best research you have . . . is based on this version of the model," Kemple said. He called Vallas's decision "changing horses midstream," and said that when decisions are not made based on evidence they result in districts implementing the "reform du jour."

Rather than attempt to fix the large neighborhood high schools, Vallas's plan was to create alternatives to them. He started twenty-six new small schools, backed the creation of more charter schools, and created disciplinary schools that were run on contract by private companies. As of 2002, there were thirty-eight public high schools in Philadelphia, with an average enrollment of 1,700 students. By 2007, there were sixty-two schools, including charters. Today there are ninety, twenty-nine of them charters.

New Research

As Vallas was deciding to move away from Talent Development, Robert Balfanz and Ruth Curran Neild, two Johns Hopkins researchers, began a retrospective study, paid for by a number of national and local foundations, of the "dropout crisis," covering the years from 2000 to 2005. Their 2006 report, called *Unfulfilled Promise*, was the first definitive counting of high school dropouts in the district, after decades of policies aimed at stemming the tide. They found that, during the period studied, some 30,000 Philadelphia students had dropped out, and thousands more were "near dropouts" who showed up less than half the time. On a positive note, however, they found evidence of improvement. More than 52 percent of the class of 2005 graduated on time in four years. That was about 4 percentage points higher than the average for the previous four years.

Until that study, "[w]e didn't have a public fix on who was dropping out, where they were dropping out from, and what kind of services they need," said Neild. Because it was one of the first studies to define the graduation rate in terms of cohorts—tracing the fortunes of each entering ninth-grade class and showing how many graduate—"it helped people realize the scale of it," she said.

The researchers discovered that many of those most likely to drop out could be identified beginning in the sixth grade and nearly all of them by the ninth grade. They advised that high schools alone could not fix the problem. The middle school grades would have to do a better job of educating their students. Keeping ninth graders on track needed to be a priority. Also important, however, was that one in five dropouts were older students who had either quit school or entered the juvenile justice system a few credits short of a diploma. The researchers recommended the creation of alternative institutions instead of expecting these youths to reenter the high schools they had already given up on. This had the potential to bump up the graduation rate quickly without dealing with the messy politics and adult interests that come with the territory in high school reform efforts.

When Paul Vallas (pictured) became the head of the Philadelphia school system, which the state had declared academically and fiscally bankrupt, he replaced the school board with a reform commission.

Project U-Turn

Not surprisingly, it was this last recommendation that Vallas seized on, because it was consistent with what he was already doing. There also was demand. The release of the report had marked the launch of a new advocacy group called the Project

U-Turn Collaborative that would help implement some of these recommendations. In the first year after its October 2006 launch, Project U-Turn raised $10 million from public and private sources, and 1,500 dropouts contacted the project to ask for help in getting a diploma. But seats could only be found for 158 in the city's existing alternative schools. Vallas created the Office of Multiple Pathways to Graduation to expand programs for disengaged youth. He contracted with private companies to run "accelerated" schools that could help students graduate more quickly. Arlene Ackerman succeeded Vallas in 2008, and she has added seats to the network, which now can accommodate 2,200 youths. Under Ackerman the district has also set up a Re-engagement Center, where former students can come and be referred to a school within the expanding network of options. And with funding from the U.S. Department of Labor, Philadelphia community organizations are now helping students who have dropped out earn either a GED or credits toward a diploma.

Renaissance Schools

The traditional high schools have not been abandoned by the new wave of reformers. Since Project U-Turn was created, the city has won about $65 million in grants, also from the Labor Department, for programs in seven neighborhood high schools that were cited as "persistently dangerous." Using some of this money, the district is creating in most of its neighborhood schools "bridge" programs that try to engage ninth graders in the summer before high school, reviving a practice first introduced by Clayton in the late '80s. Ackerman has a new plan called Renaissance Schools in which some of the worst schools will be converted to charters or slated for turnaround treatment within the district, some directly under her supervision. In the first year, three long-troubled high schools made that list.

Though disentangling the effects of all these policies on the city's overall dropout rate isn't easy, the numbers are certainly moving in the right direction. Between 2005 and 2009 the percentage of students who entered ninth grade and graduated in four years increased from 52 percent to 56 percent. And the six-year graduation rate has been steadily inching up—from 57 percent for the class of 2005 to 60 percent for the class of 2007. At least some of that six-year graduation rate increase is attributable to the new "accelerated" schools, according to Project U-Turn data.

It could be that Vallas and Project U-Turn are right and that taking on dysfunctional high schools was too hard and expensive, at least at the time. But there's a limit to what the alternative schools Vallas and Ackerman have encouraged can do: most of the students entering them have accumulated very few high school credits and have reading and math proficiency that hovers around the fifth-grade level.

Even with the improvements, each year more than 8,000 Philadelphia students drop out, most from the neighborhood schools. Project U-Turn's goal is to cut that number by at least 2,000 students by the end of the upcoming school year [2010–2011]. Philadelphia Mayor Michael Nutter has set a high bar as well. He has committed city resources to increasing the six-year graduation rate to 80 percent. To reach those audacious goals, Philadelphia will need to do what it hasn't succeeded in doing in the past—fix neighborhood schools. And with the Obama administration now pledging billions of federal dollars for school "turnaround" efforts, Philadelphia has another opportunity to keep trying.

ELEVEN

Blended Learning Offers High School Dropouts a Second Chance

June Kronholz

Whereas many programs are designed to keep students in school, new approaches are also being created to give students who have already made the decision to leave school a second chance at graduation. June Kronholz, a former *Wall Street Journal* foreign correspondent, bureau chief, and education reporter, and currently a contributing editor at *Education Next*, describes one such second-chance high school. The school uses blended learning, which combines online and classroom instruction. Kronholz explains how and why the program seems to be successful.

Eighteen-year-old Tyriq was fairly blunt about the mess he had gotten himself into before transferring to the Hampton, Virginia, online school where I approached him one chilly day this spring [2011]. "I got in trouble. I was playing around. I got backed up" in high school, he said. He had failed three classes in his junior year and, faced with the prospect of repeating a year, probably would have dropped out instead, he told me. "I didn't want that kind of pressure."

People who deal with at-risk teenagers say dropping out is not an event; it's a process. Youngsters miss school and get "backed up" in class, so they miss more school because they're bewildered or embarrassed, and fall further behind. Seeing few ways to recover, "they just silently drop out," said Richard Firth, who showed me around the Hampton school and two others in Richmond that are using online learning to derail the cycle.

In the three years the 75-seat Hampton Performance Learning Center [PLC] has been open, it claims to have graduated 91 students. There's a waiting list for admission, so the school opened a second shift, which also is near capacity. Sherri Pritchard, the school's social-studies "learning facilitator"—there are no teachers and no principal here—said 95 percent of her online students pass Virginia's end-of-course history test, which would put them well ahead of both the Hampton school district's and state's pass rates.

And Tyriq: He has only a C average after a year at the Hampton PLC, he said, but he graduated in June—on time—and plans to enlist in the Army, his goal all along. . . .

Almost disarmingly, the PLCs reach out to youngsters that schools typically find the most troublesome. Sherman Curl, the academic coordinator—i.e., principal—at the Adult Career Development Center PLC in Richmond, handed me a brochure describing the students for whom the PLC is a good fit; kids with "poor attendance," "excessive tardiness," "academic failure," "apathy," "social issues," low motivation, and such "challenges to success" as pregnancy and poverty, it read.

In a summary of its 2009–10 academic year, Virginia's Communities in Schools reported that one-third of the students at its four PLCs were at least two years behind in academic credits when they arrived. They were a year or two older than their conventional-school peers and, in the previous year, averaged six suspensions and 24 absences each at their former schools. Several youngsters told me they'd fallen in with the wrong crowd at their old schools, or they felt bullied and isolated. "I started messing up," a chatty 18-year-old named Chelsie Saunders told me at the Hampton PLC, which is housed in a modern teen center, complete

Blended learning uses online courses to give dropouts and near-dropouts a second chance at graduation.

with pool tables, a basketball court, a coffee bar, and an airy television lounge with leather sofas.

"These are kids who never made it in a comprehensive school," said Wes Hamner, the academic coordinator at the Richmond Technical Center PLC, which occupies one floor of a sprawling trades-training campus in Richmond's industrial district.

For all that, the three PLCs I visited were remarkably quiet and orderly: There wasn't much chatter about what kids were learning, but there wasn't any catcalling, hallway scuffling, or acting out in class, either. Hamner pointed out that there's no security at his school and that the lockers don't even have locks. Teachers sat in the back or in a corner of the classrooms, while students sat at computers, wearing headsets.

Teaching to the Student

At Hampton, I asked Pritchard, the social-studies facilitator, how she knew what her students were doing, so she opened a dashboard on her computer. It showed that on computer 3, a student was working on a U.S. history unit, or "module," on civil rights. The teenager on computer 6 was working on a module on imperialism for the same course, and the student on computer 7 was doing a review and practice test on the executive branch of the U.S. government.

Most PLCs, including those in Virginia, use NovaNET, an online curriculum that is marketed by Pearson Education Inc. The program tests a student at the end of each lesson, module, and course, and lets those who pass their tests with at least an 80 percent move on. For those who don't pass, the computer singles out the content they seemed not to understand, reteaches it, and retests.

Kids like the immediate feedback, Katherine Fox, the academic coordinator at Hampton, told me: "It's difficult for them to wait for success. Kids want to move on." A mop-haired boy named Michael told me that he used to obsess over test questions at his conventional school and couldn't force himself to move ahead. The NovaNET practice tests and make-up tests relieved him of that anxiety, he said, as he pulled certificates from his backpack to show that he had completed two business classes, oceanography, and biology. "No one gets left behind here," he said.

Back on Pritchard's dashboard, meanwhile, I could see that the student on computer 1 was using an open-source educational website called SAS Curriculum Pathways to research voting rights for the government class, while the student on computer 2 was researching Appomattox on SAS for history class. Most Hampton PLC computers can access only NovaNET; the few that can access SAS can't go any further than research sites to which SAS provides a link.

At the career center PLC in Richmond, which is housed on the top floor of a 1920s-era school built for the city's elite black students, science facilitator Patricia Sessions showed me more. A "pacing sheet," a sort of minimum speed limit set by the state education department, suggested that teachers should expect to devote three weeks to a unit on biochemical processes, part of the biology curriculum. But when Sessions opened the computer file of a student named Trish, it showed that Trish had finished the unit in a week. She'd spent 26 minutes on an online lesson about atoms and molecules, and got a 90 on the test. She'd spent an hour on the properties-of-water lesson and another hour on acids and bases, and got 80 on both.

Teachers told me that most NovaNET courses are comparable to textbook-based courses in length and content—a comeback to critics who talk of watered-down curricula at alternative schools—but that many students move through them more quickly, and often finish high school a semester early. "I'm constantly working rather than waiting," explained a tattooed girl named Shaina at the Richmond Tech school.

Pritchard told me that she started the school year with students grouped largely by subject—say, geography in one period, government in another. But as the year went on, and students progressed at different speeds, classes became more diverse. In any class period now, she could have youngsters working on either semester of any of four subjects.

As students finish courses, they can move to another classroom to work on courses they may find slower going. If they earn enough credits to graduate before the school year is over, the services coordinator steers them to mentorships, trade training, or jobs. Sessions, who was playing [music by classical composer Felix] Mendelssohn in her otherwise-silent classroom as her students worked, said she started the year with 20 kids in her afternoon class and was down to 8 by late March.

All that movement precludes lectures or class discussions. Teachers told me that anywhere from 60 to 90 percent of the work in their classrooms is done online, with work sheets, projects, one-on-one meetings, and, for seniors, a research report and presenta-

Dropouts Did Not Feel Motivated or Inspired to Work Hard

Blended and online learning provides immediate feedback which can be motivating for many students.

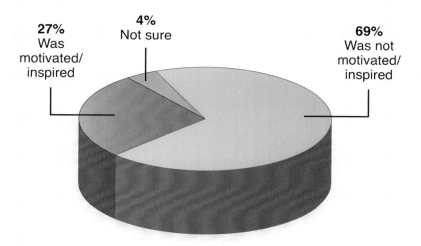

27%
Was
motivated/
inspired

4%
Not sure

69%
Was not
motivated/
inspired

Taken from: John M. Bridgeland, John J. Dilulio Jr. and Karen Burke Morrison. "The Silent Epidemic: Perspectives of High School Dropouts," March 2006.

tion accounting for the rest. The walls of Pritchard's classroom were ringed with poster-board projects on the Zhou Dynasty, the Battle of Fort Fisher, and the roles of the secretary of defense and the U.S. Department of Education, among others. It wasn't AP [advanced placement] material, perhaps, but it showed persistence and attention to detail that are not always common in city schools. Last year, the whole school read the same book, *Facing the Lion*, and used it as a springboard for cross-disciplinary studies.

The students I talked with said they didn't miss discussions or were self-aware enough to know that lectures didn't fit their learning style. "I wouldn't be listening anyway," Tyriq told me; "I'm not a person to talk," said another 18-year-old named Dashawn. Instead, kids said they liked the anonymity and independence of working online. "I like being in my own bubble," Chelsie Saunders told me in Hampton: "I don't like waiting on people" on some lessons and "I don't worry about people getting frustrated with me" for working slowly on others.

A Promising Start

The PLCs take youngsters who have at least attempted 9th grade, plus a few overage 8th graders. But most kids arrive in 10th or 11th grade when they realize they're not on track to graduate. For admission, they must score at an 8th-grade level on standardized reading and math tests (the Richmond Tech PLC raised that to 9th grade because it had so many applicants), pass an interview, and sign an achievement contract that also commits them to attend a daily meeting called Morning Motivation. Each gets a learning plan that plots an individual path to graduation and then to a trade program, a job, or college. . . .

Credit-recovery and online programs have been accused of low standards and a weak-tea curriculum, anything to get kids into the graduation statistics, critics contend. But the PLCs insist on the rigor of their program because it's based on a general-education curriculum, not a credit-recovery curriculum. PLC students take the same state tests as their traditional-school peers. And computer testing on NovaNET and other online curricula prevents social promotion or the intervention of soft-hearted administrators. "We legally graduate kids; I don't do them any favors," said Wes Hamner at Richmond Tech PLC.

In a report on the 2009–10 school year, the project says that, nationally, its students improved their scores in all four core subjects compared to their performance in their home school the year before—by from 6 to 11 percentage points—and that 96 percent of the students classified as seniors at the beginning of the school year graduated. For a project that works with potential dropouts, that's hugely impressive, but there has been little outside research on the PLCs that would confirm that. . . .

Still, more than one-third of the youngsters who started at the Virginia PLCs in fall 2009 graduated in 2010, including 68 students who headed to two- or four-year colleges, the Virginia project reported.

When I spoke with Chelsie Saunders in Hampton in early spring, she laid out a career path that included community college, university, and then a career in teaching or nursing. "Honestly, if it wasn't for here, I wouldn't graduate," she told me. When I checked back in June, she had.

What You Should Know About Dropping Out of School

The Dropout Rate Has Decreased

The National Center for Educational Statistics (NCES), defines the dropout rate as the percentage of sixteen- to twenty-four-year-olds who are not attending high school, have not earned a high school diploma or a General Educational Development (GED) certificate, and are not incarcerated. According to the NCES:

- Between 1980 and 2009, the overall dropout rate in the United States has decreased fairly steadily, dropping from 14 percent in 1980 to about 8 percent in 2009.
- The period of most significant decline occurred between 2000 and 2009, when the dropout rate fell from 11 percent to 8 percent.
- The dropout rate decreased substantially for all races and ethnicities during this period.

The Dropout Rate Is Higher Among Certain Segments of the Population

According to the NCES:

- Black and Hispanic young people are much more likely than non-Hispanic whites to drop out of high school. In 2009 the dropout rate for whites was at 5 percent, for blacks 10 percent, and for Hispanics 18 percent. Asians are the most likely to graduate, with a dropout rate of only 2 percent.

- Boys are more likely to drop out of school than girls, 9 percent versus 7 percent. Boys make up 50 percent of the population, but account for 57 percent of nongraduates.
- Teen mothers are far more likely to drop out of school. Only 50 percent of teen mothers graduated or earned a GED by the time they were twenty-two years old, compared with 90 percent of women who were not mothers, according to a 2010 Child Trends Databank report.
- Youth with disabilities are almost twice as likely to drop out of school, at a rate of 15.5 percent versus about 8 percent.
- Youth from low-income families are far more likely to drop out of school, at a rate of 16.7 percent versus 3.2 percent.

Dropout Rates Need to Be Viewed in Context

According to the Child Trends Databank:
- The decreased dropout rate among African American men is due in part to their record-high rates of incarceration, which doubled between 1980 and 1999; these individuals are not counted among dropouts.
- The high dropout rate among Hispanic youth is due in part to the inclusion of immigrants in this age range who never attended high school in the United States (so, technically, they did not drop out of school; they never went in the first place).

Dropping Out of School Has Negative Financial Consequences

According to 2010 US Census figures, educational attainment directly relates to average yearly income. The annual income made by those who have earned various degrees is shown as follows:
- advanced degree: $83,841
- bachelor's degree: $57,621
- some college / associate's degree: $34,366
- high school graduate: $31,003
- not a high school graduate: $20,911

What You Should Do About Dropping Out of School

In the United States, seven thousand high school students drop out of school every day. One out of every four high school freshmen will not graduate with his or her class. More than 8 percent of sixteen- to twenty-four-year-olds are considered high school dropouts. What can one student do to improve graduation rates?

Graduation and dropout rates vary significantly among communities and individual schools. For example, for public schools in Michigan about 75 percent of students beginning high school in 2006 graduated with their classes in 2010. Statewide, the lowest and highest performing districts ranged from less than 25 percent graduating to 100 percent graduating. Detroit City School District, the largest district in Michigan, averaged about 62 percent, whereas individual high schools in Detroit ranged from under 25 percent to over 95 percent.

Know the graduation rates for your state, city, and your own school and whether those rates are improving or getting worse. The No Child Left Behind Act requires all public schools and districts to report graduation rates, so this information should be available at your state's website. Additionally, most school districts publish some kind of annual report that should include statistics and what the district is doing to improve graduation rates. Find out the dropout rate for your community and attend school board meetings where you can cheer your leaders on or ask them to do more. Arrange to speak at the meeting and give your perspective as a student.

Reach Out

In a 2006 report, the top five reasons students gave for dropping out of school were: (1) uninteresting classes, (2) hopelessly behind because of absences, (3) hanging out with people not interested in school, (4) too much freedom and not enough boundaries in life, and (5) failing their classes.

Because of the power of peer pressure, you as a student are in a unique position to help your classmates overcome some of these obstacles. Notice when people are missing from class and help them if you can; they might need someone to keep them up-to-date on assignments. Be that friend who is interested in school that they can hang out with. Even spending time together studying outside of class can help someone stay on track. Some of the best words used to beat the dropout crisis at your school might be, "Hey, do you want to hang out and do homework?" Finally, if your school has a peer tutoring program, volunteer. If it doesn't, encourage the principal to start one.

Stop Bullying

Some of the reasons that students list for dropping out of school can be directly caused by bullying. If someone is afraid to go to school or to a particular class, of course he or she will fall behind. Other students may drop out directly due to bullying. According to the National Association of School Principals, only 25 percent of teachers view bullying as a problem, and they only intervene in about 4 percent of bullying incidents. If your school does not have an antibullying group, ask that one be started. If it does have one, become involved.

Spend Time

According to the National Dropout Prevention Center Network, one of the most important things that researchers have found regarding the prevention of high school dropouts is that early childhood education (preschool) is the best way to reduce a child's risk of dropping out if the child otherwise has the odds stacked against him or her. Furthermore, according to the Progressive Policy Institute, there is an 80 percent correlation between being two years behind in reading level in fourth grade and dropping out of high school. Spending time reading to or with small children, helping them read, or even just sharing fun reading material is one thing that you can do about preventing kids from dropping out of school.

Beat the Odds

The odds of not making it to graduation are definitely higher for some groups of people. You might already be in tune with your odds simply by being in tune with your family, school, and neighborhood. Just because the odds may not be in your favor, however, does not mean that you cannot beat them.

In the book *We Beat the Street: How a Friendship Pact Led to Success,* Sampson Davis, George Jenkins, and Rameck Hunt tell how as teens in high school they promised each other that they would not succumb to the streets of their rough Newark, New Jersey, neighborhood but would graduate from high school, go to college and medical school, and become doctors. They kept their promises, helping each other—and themselves—along the way and are now doctors and a dentist. Whether you live in a tough neighborhood or not, you need positive influences, and other students need positive influences, too. Set goals, celebrate small and large accomplishments, and be a friend, helping your peers set goals that will help keep you all on track to graduation.

The editors have compiled the following list of organizations concerned with the issues debated in this book. The descriptions are derived from materials provided by the organizations. All have publications or information available for interested readers. The list was compiled on the date of publication of the present volume; names, addresses, phone and fax numbers, and e-mail and Internet addresses may change. Be aware that many organizations take several weeks or longer to respond to inquiries, so allow as much time as possible.

Advancement Project
1220 L St. NW, Ste. 850, Washington, DC 20005
(202) 728-9557 • fax: (202) 728-9558
website: www.advancementproject.org

Advancement Project is a policy, communications, and legal action group committed to racial justice that was founded by a team of veteran civil rights lawyers in 1999. It partners with community organizations to bring them the tools of legal advocacy and strategic communications in order to dismantle structural exclusion, including the school-to-prison pipeline. Its online library includes reports, news, legal memos, litigation, and court testimony.

Alliance for Excellent Education
1201 Connecticut Ave. NW, Ste. 901, Washington, DC 20036
(202) 828 0828 • fax: (202) 828 0821
website: www.all4ed.org

The Alliance for Excellent Education is a national policy and advocacy organization that works to improve national and federal policy so that all students can achieve at high academic levels and graduate from high school ready for success in college, work, and citizenship in the twenty-first century. To encourage public awareness and action that support effective secondary school reform, the alliance publishes many briefs, reports, and fact sheets and publishes a biweekly newsletter, *Straight A's*, which provides in an accessible format information on public education policy and progress.

American Civil Liberties Union (ACLU)

125 Broad St., New York, NY 10005
(212) 549-2900
e-mail: www.aclu.org/general-feedback
website: www.aclu.org

The ACLU is a national organization that works to defend Americans' civil rights as guaranteed by the US Constitution. The ACLU is working to guarantee all students equal access to educational opportunities and resources in an educational environment free from gender-based stereotypes, violence, and harassment. Among the ACLU's numerous publications are fact sheets such as, "Gender-Based Violence and Harrassment: Your School Your Rights" and resources such as LGBT Youth and Schools Resources and Links.

America's Promise Alliance

1110 Vermont Ave. NW, Ste. 900, Washington, DC 20005
(202) 657-0600 • fax (202) 657-0601
e-mail: info@americaspromise.org
website: www.americaspromise.org

The goal of America's Promise Alliance is to ensure that all young people graduate from high school ready for college, work, and life through its Grad Nation movement. Its work involves driving awareness, creating connections, and sharing knowledge to provide children the Five Promises: (1) caring adults, (2) safe places, (3) a healthy start, (4) an effective education, and (5) opportunities to help others. Research, reports, partner resources, and interactive tools are available at its website, including its annual report, "Building a Grad Nation: Progress and Challenge in Ending the High School Dropout Epidemic."

Children's Defense Fund (CDF)

25 E St. NW, Washington, DC 20001

(800) 233-1200

e-mail: cdfinfo@childrensdefense.org

website: childrensdefense.org

CDF is a nonprofit child advocacy organization that has worked for over thirty-five years to ensure a level playing field for all children. It champions policies and programs that lift children out of poverty; protect them from abuse and neglect; and ensure their access to health care, quality education, and a moral and spiritual foundation.

Fresh Lifelines for Youth (FLY)

568 Valley Way, Milpitas, CA 95035

(408) 263-2630

e-mail: http://flyprogram.org/contact/

website: www.flyprogram.org

FLY encourages teens in trouble to make healthy decisions by offering at-risk and disadvantaged youth mentoring and leadership training programs. The group advocates education, attention, and mentoring as the best ways to keep kids in school and out of prison.

National Dropout Prevention Center/Network

Clemson University, 209 Martin St., Clemson, SC 29631-1555

(864) 656-2599

e-mail: ndpc@clemson.edu

website: www.dropoutprevention.org

The mission of the National Dropout Prevention Center/Network is to increase high school graduation rates through research and evidence-based solutions. It conducts conferences, seminars, and program evaluations and provides informational resources through its website, including radio webcasts, newsletters, a resource library, major research reports, family/student resources, grant resources, and its journal, *At-Risk*.

National Dropout Prevention Center
for Students with Disabilities
Clemson University, 209 Martin St., Clemson, SC 29631-1555
(866) 745-5641 • TDD: (866) 212-2775
e-mail: ndpcsd-l@clemson.edu
website: www.ndpc-sd.org

The ultimate goal of the National Dropout Prevention Center for Students with Disabilities is to provide high-quality, evidence-based technical assistance to help states build and implement sustainable programs and best practices that will yield positive results in dropout prevention, reentry, and school completion for students with disabilities. Available through the organization's website is a variety of resources for state and local education agencies, as well as for practitioners and parents. There are also links to dropout-related reports.

Office of Juvenile Justice and Delinquency Prevention (OJJDP)
810 Seventh St. NW, Washington, DC 20531
(202) 307-5911 • fax: (202) 307-2093
e-mail: askjj@ncjrs.org
website: ojjdp.ncjrs.org

The OJJDP provides national leadership, coordination, and resources to prevent and respond to juvenile delinquency and victimization. OJJDP supports states and communities in their efforts to develop and implement prevention and intervention programs and to improve the juvenile justice system so that it protects public safety, holds offenders accountable, and provides treatment and rehabilitative services tailored to the needs of juveniles and their families. OJJDP publishes the journal *Juvenile Justice* and other publications, such as "A Parent's Guide to Truancy," and OJJDP Bulletins, with topics such as "Truancy Reduction: Keeping Students in School."

Voices for America's Children
1000 Vermont Ave. NW, Ste. 700, Washington, DC 20005
(202) 289-0777

e-mail: voices@voices.org
website: www.voicesforamericaschildren.org

Voices for America's Children is a network of child advocacy groups. It seeks to maximize the effectiveness of such groups in their key policy goals of equity, health, school readiness, school success, safety, and economic stability. The website offers a database of publications on topics such as education, juvenile justice, child poverty, and community mobilization.

BIBLIOGRAPHY

Books

John M. Bridgeland, John J. DiIulio Jr., and Karen Burke Morison, *The Silent Epidemic: Perspectives of High School Dropouts.* Washington, DC: Civic Enterprises, March 2006.

Steven Brill, *Class Warfare: Inside the Fight to Fix America's Schools.* New York: Simon & Schuster, 2011.

Linda Darling-Hammond, *The Flat World and Education: How America's Commitment to Equity Will Determine Our Future.* New York: Teachers College Press, 2010.

Sampson Davis, George Jenkins, and Rameck Hunt, *The Pact: Three Young Men Make a Promise and Fulfill a Dream.* New York: Riverhead, 2002.

———, *We Beat the Street: How a Friendship Pact Helped Us Succeed.* New York: Dutton Children's, 2005.

Guy Garcia, *The Decline of Men: How the American Male Is Tuning Out, Giving Up, and Flipping Off His Future.* New York: HarperCollins, 2008.

Jonathan Kozol, *The Shame of the Nation: The Restoration of Apartheid Schooling in America.* New York: Crown, 2005.

Laura Longhine and Keith Hefner, *Real Men, Real Stories: Urban Teens Write About How to Be a Man.* New York: Youth Communication, 2010.

Gary Orfield, *Dropouts in America: Confronting the Graduation Rate Crisis.* Cambridge, MA: Harvard Education Press, 2004.

Ruby K. Payne and Paul D. Slocumb, *Boys in Poverty: A Framework for Understanding Dropout.* Bloomington, IN: Solution Tree, 2011.

Diane Ravitch, *The Death and Life of the Great American School System: How Testing and Choice Are Undermining Education.* New York: Basic, 2010.

Russell R. Rumberger, *Dropping Out: Why Students Drop Out of High School and What Can Be Done About It*. Cambridge, MA: Harvard University Press, 2011.

Tavis Smiley, *Too Important to Fail: Saving America's Boys: Tavis Smiley Reports*. New York: Smiley, 2011.

Periodicals and Internet Sources

American Psychological Association, "Facing the School Dropout Dilemma," www.apa.org/pi/families/resources/school-dropout-prevention.aspx.

John Bridgeland, "The Key to Keeping Teens in School," *Christian Science Monitor*, April 15, 2008.

Child Trends Data Bank, "High School Dropout Rates: Indicators on Children and Youth," February 2011. www.childtrendsdatabank.org/sites/default/files/01_Dropout_Rates_0.pdf.

Greg J. Duncan and Richard J. Murnane, "Economic Inequality: The Real Cause of the Urban School Problem," *Chicago Tribune*, October 6, 2011.

Gay, Lesbian and Straight Education Network, "The 2009 School Climate Survey: The Experiences of Lesbian, Gay, Bisexual and Transgender Youth in Our Nation's Schools," 2010. www.glsen.org/binary-data/GLSEN_ATTACHMENTS/file/000/001/1675-2.pdf.

Lois Kazakoff, "Raising Dropout Age Isn't Enough," *San Francisco Chronicle*, February 6, 2012.

June Kronholz, "The Challenges of Keeping Kids in School," *Education Next*, Winter 2011.

Kyle M. McCallumore and Ervin F. Sparapani, "The Importance of the Ninth Grade on High School Graduation Rates and Student Success in High School," *Education*, October, 2010.

Kathy Mulady, "Zero Tolerance Kills Dreams, Hurts the Economy," Nation of Change, December 3, 2011. www.nationofchange.org/school-zero-tolerance-kills-dreams-hurts-economy-1322924527.

Susan Reese, "Advocacy on the Front Lines of CTE (Career Technical Education)," *Techniques*, September 2011.

Anastasia R. Snyder and Diane K. McLaughlin, "Rural Youth Are More Likely to Be Idle," *Carsey Institute Fact Sheet No. 11*, Winter 2008. www.carseyinstitute.unh.edu/publications /FS_RuralYouth_08.pdf.

USA Today, "18 Is Not the Answer," February 15, 2011.

———, "In Today's Economy, Age 16 Is Too Soon to Drop Out of School," February 15, 2012.

Terry Wilhelm, "Come Back Kids: This Program Seeks Out Dropouts Who Had No Plans to Re-Enroll and Offers Them a Flexible, Personalized Educational Environment That Leads to a Diploma and a Plan for the Future," *Leadership*, November– December 2009.